Utilize este código QR para se cadastrar de forma mais rápida:

Ou, se preferir, entre em:
www.richmond.com.br/ac/livroportal
e siga as instruções para ter acesso aos conteúdos exclusivos do
Portal e Livro Digital

CÓDIGO DE ACESSO:
P 00144 JBEANS 1 21646

Faça apenas um cadastro. Ele será válido para:

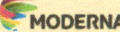 

De los árboles a los libros,
sostenibilidad en todo el camino

Da semente ao livro,
sustentabilidade por todo o caminho

Plantar bosques
La madera usada como materia prima para nuestro papel viene de plantaciones renovables, o sea, no es fruto de deforestación. Este tipo de plantación genera millares de empleos para los agricultores y ayuda a recuperar las áreas ambientales degradadas.

Plantar florestas
A madeira que serve de matéria-prima para nosso papel vem de plantio renovável, ou seja, não é fruto de desmatamento. Essa prática gera milhares de empregos para agricultores e ajuda a recuperar áreas ambientais degradadas.

Fabricar papel e imprimir libros
Toda la cadena de producción de papel, desde la fabricación de la celulosa hasta la encuadernación del libro, tiene los correspondientes certificados y cumple los patrones internacionales de procesamiento sostenible y las buenas prácticas ambientales.

Fabricar papel e imprimir livros
Toda a cadeia produtiva do papel, desde a produção de celulose até a encadernação do livro, é certificado, cumprindo padrões internacionais de processamento sustentável e boas práticas ambientais.

Crear contenido
Los profesionales involucrados en la elaboración de nuestras soluciones educativas tienen como objetivo una educación para la vida basada en la curaduría editorial, la diversidad de visiones y la responsabilidad socioambiental.

Criar conteúdo
Os profissionais envolvidos na elaboração de nossas soluções educacionais buscam uma educação para a vida pautada por curadoria editorial, diversidade de olhares e responsabilidade socioambiental.

Construir proyectos de vida
Ofrecer una solución educativa Santillana Español es un acto de compromiso con el futuro de las nuevas generaciones y posibilita una alianza entre las escuelas y las familias en la misión de educar.

Construir projetos de vida
Oferecer uma solução educacional Santillana Español é um ato de comprometimento com o futuro das novas gerações, possibilitando uma relação de parceria entre escolas e famílias na missão de educar!

Apoio:
www.twosides.org.br

Para saber más, escanea el código QR.
Accede a *http://mod.lk/sostenab*

Fotografe o código QR e conheça melhor esse caminho.
Saiba mais em *http://mod.lk/sostenab*

Point and color.

Unit 1   **I can do it**   Lesson 1

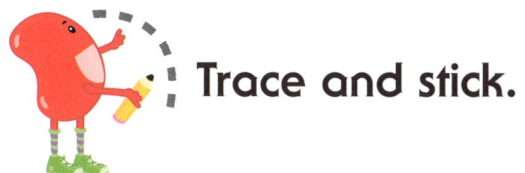

Trace and stick.

Unit 1 **I can do it** Lesson 1

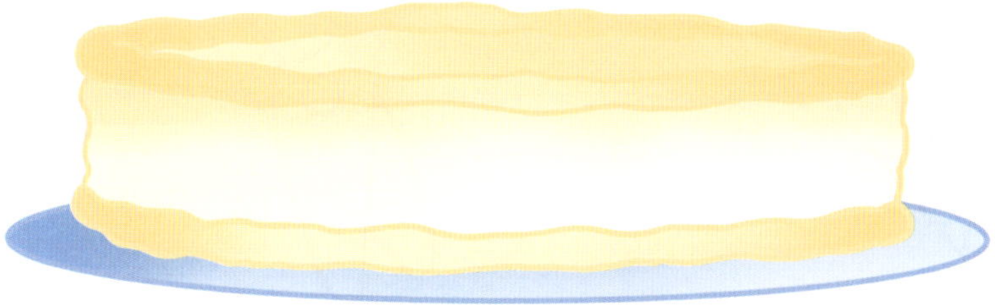

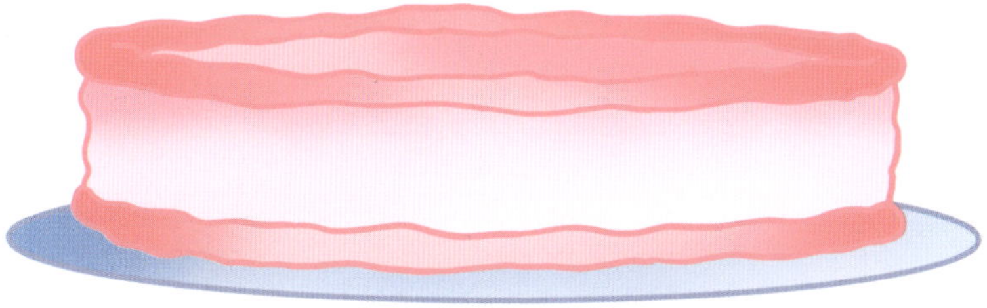

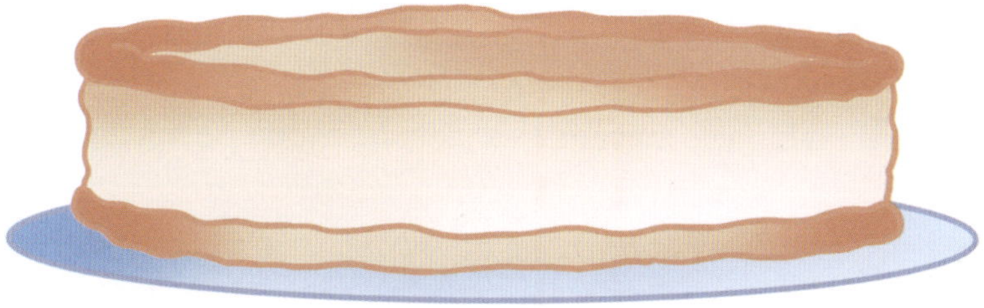

 Trace, stick and color.

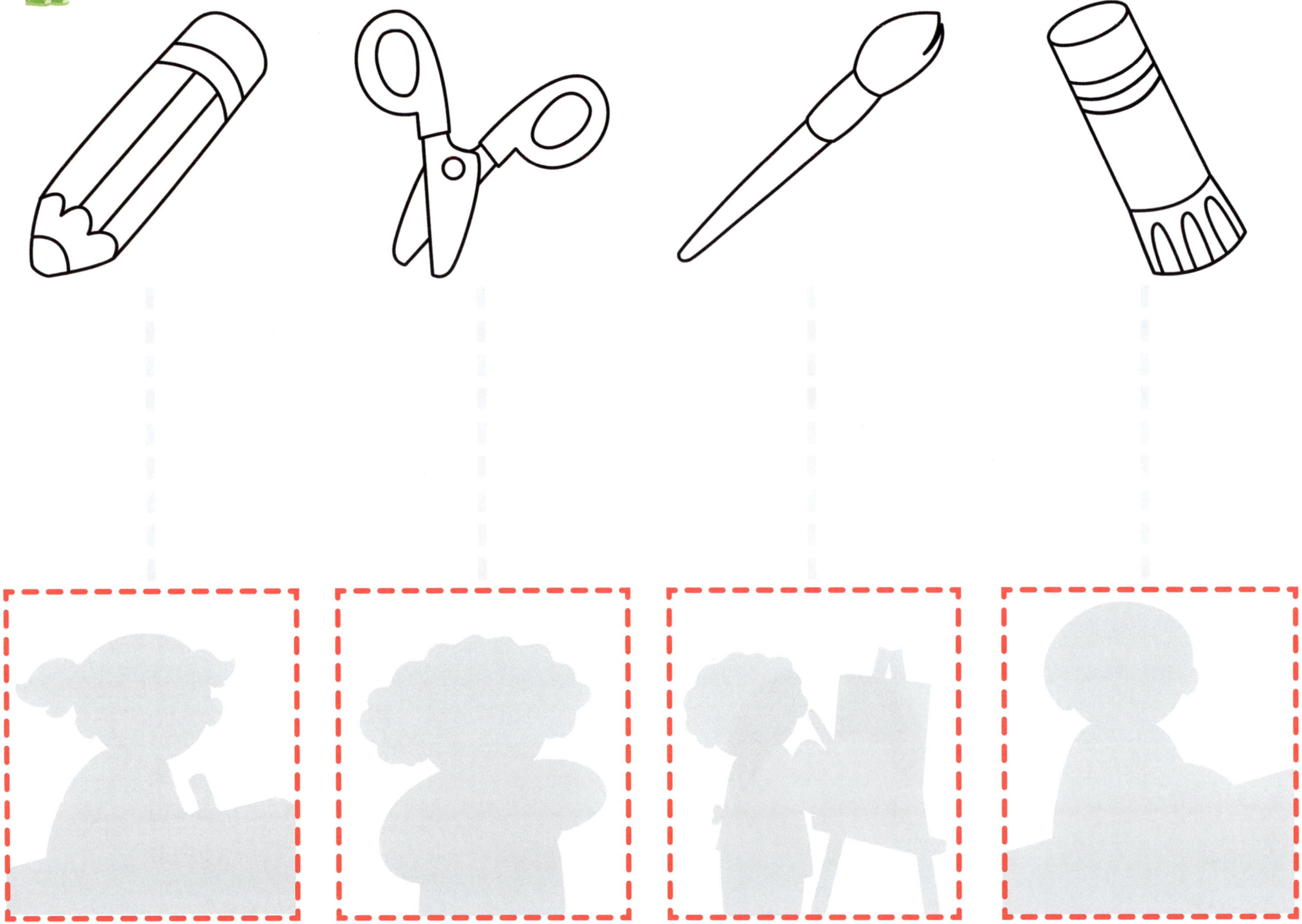

Unit 1   I can do it   Lesson 2

 Trace and draw.

Unit 1   **I can do it**   Lesson 2

One bug, two bugs

Unit 2

Look and color.

Unit 2 One bug, two bugs   Lesson 1

Look and stick.

 Look and stick.

Unit 2 **One bug, two bugs** Lesson 2

Trace, match and color.

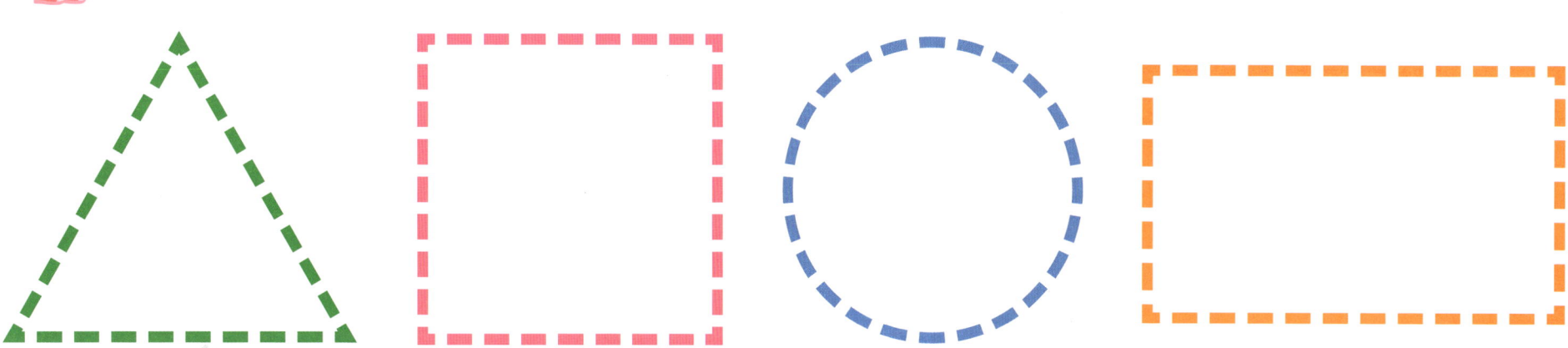

Count and color.

7 =   8 =   9 =   10 =

Trace and stick.

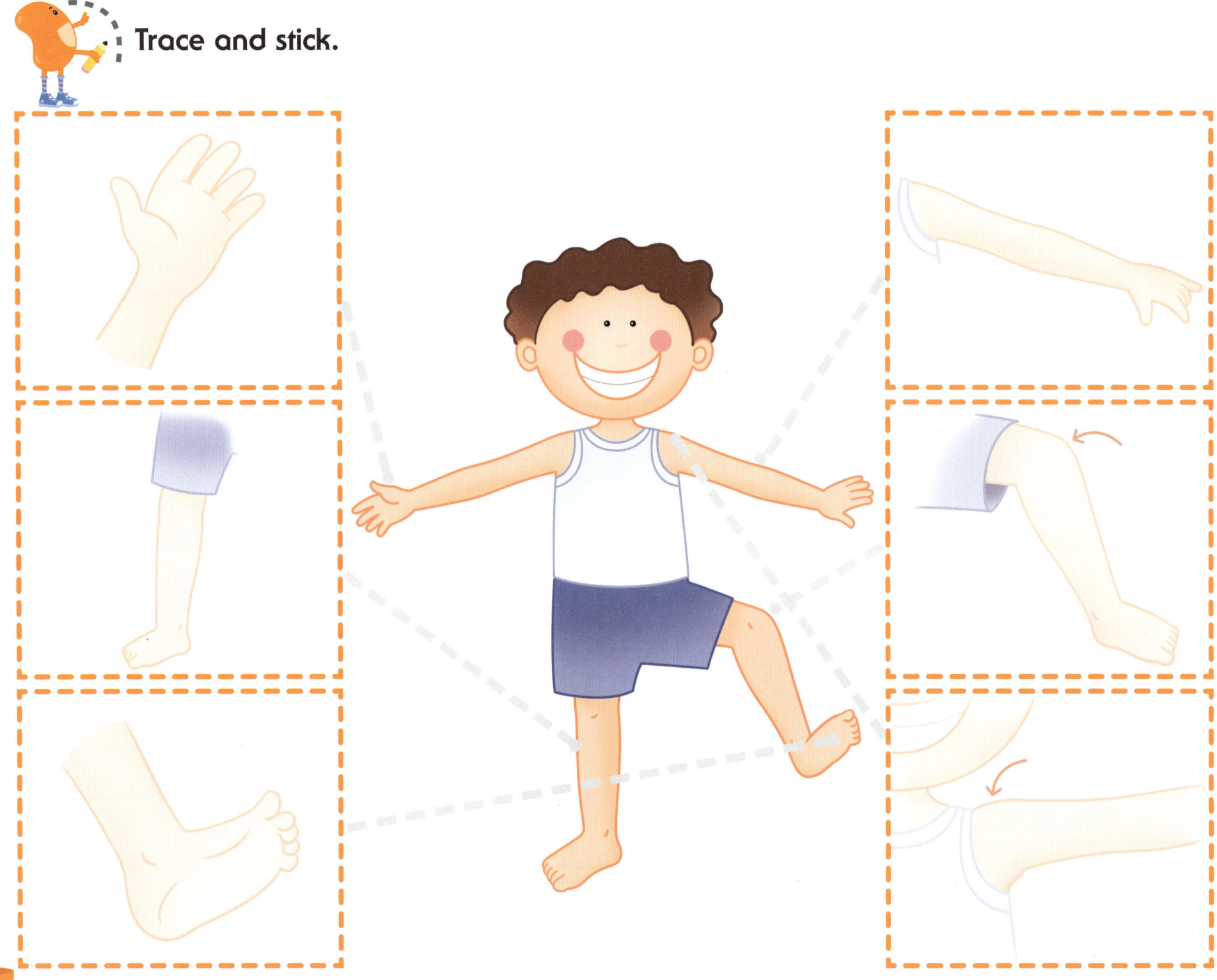

Unit 3 **My healthy body**   Lesson 1

 **Look and trace.**

Unit 3 My healthy body   Lesson 1

Trace and stick.

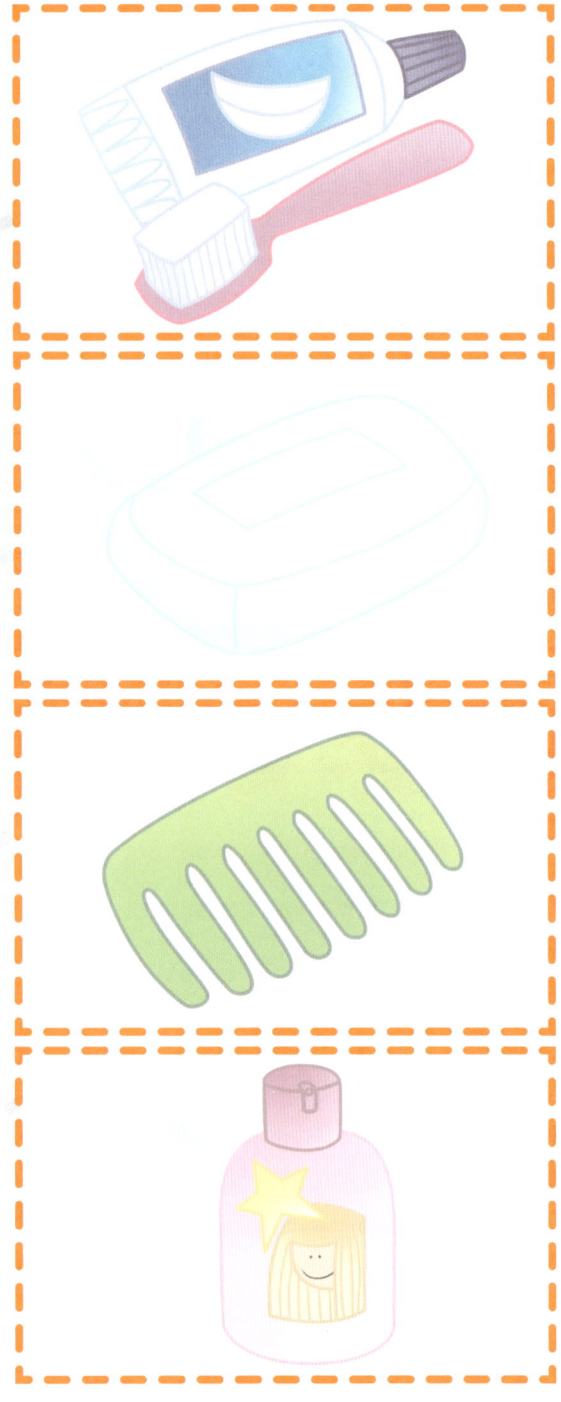

Unit 3 **My healthy body**   Lesson 2

Look and circle.

 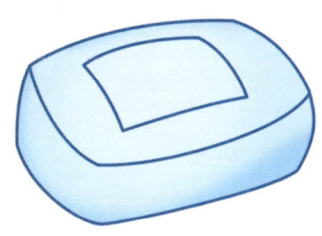  

Unit 3 My healthy body   Lesson 2

Look, match and color.

Unit 3 **My healthy body**   Review

Point and color.

Unit 4 **Busy days**   Lesson 1

Look and stick.

Unit 4 **Busy days**   Lesson 1

Look and stick.

A busy day

Unit 4 **Busy days**   Lesson 2

Look, trace and color.

 Look, match and color.

Point and stick.

Unit 5 My world   Lesson 1

Look and color.

Look, trace and stick.

Unit 5 My world   Lesson 2

Trace and color.

Look, draw and color.

My town

Unit 6

Look and stick.

Unit 6 **My town** Lesson 1

Look and color.

Unit 6 **My town** Lesson 1

Look and stick.

36 Unit 6 **My town**   Lesson 2

Look and match.

Unit 6　**My town**　　Lesson 2

Match, draw and color.

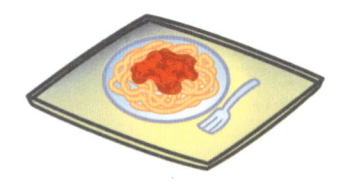

Unit 6   My town   Review

At the zoo

Unit 7

Look, stick and match.

Unit 7 At the zoo   Lesson 1

Count, trace and draw.

Unit 7 At the zoo Lesson 1

Point and stick.

Unit 7 **At the zoo** Lesson 2

Look and color.

Trace, draw and color.

Going places

Unit 8

Point and color.

Unit 8 Going places   Lesson 1

Look, count and stick.

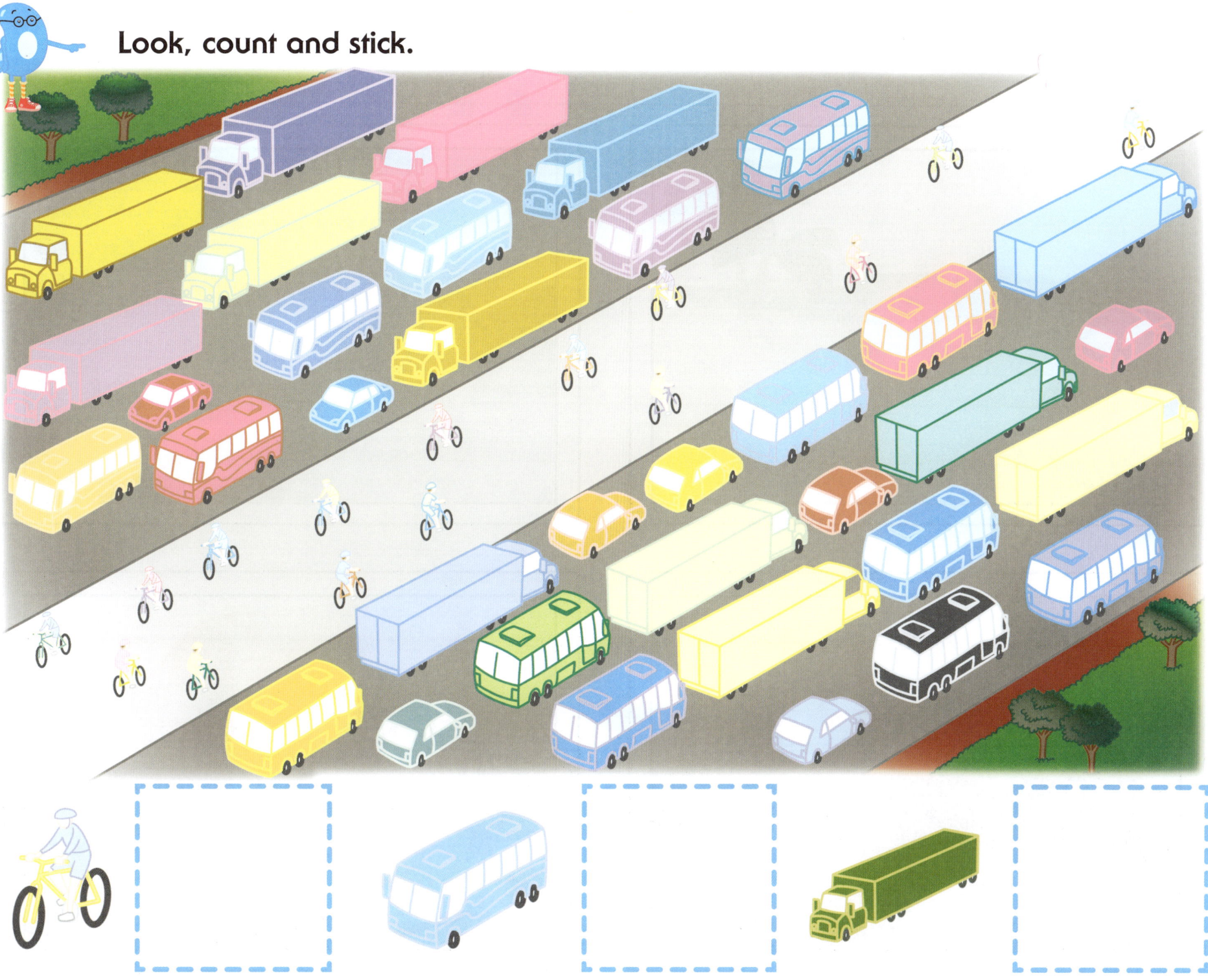

Unit 8 Going places   Lesson 1

Look and stick.

Unit 8 Going places   Lesson 2

Look, trace and color.

Look, trace and color.

50 Unit 8 **Going places** Review

Unit 1   I can do it

cut   color

draw   glue

write   paint

Unit 2   One bug, two bugs

bug   log

flowerpot   leaf

rock   garden

Picture dictionary

Unit 3   My healthy body

- shampoo
- towel
- toothbrush
- hairbrush
- soap
- comb
- toothpaste

Unit 4   Busy days

- sweep the floor
- pick up the toys
- take out the trash
- set the table
- wash the dishes
- make the bed
- feed the dog

Picture dictionary

Unit 5 My world

- mountain
- pond
- river
- squirrel
- forest

Unit 6 My town

- police officer
- firefighter
- doctor
- bus driver
- waitress
- waiter
- baker

Picture dictionary

53

Unit 7 At the zoo

- elephant
- giraffe
- lion
- hippo
- parrot
- penguin
- kangaroo
- monkey

Unit 8 Going places

- plane
- boat
- car
- bicycle
- truck
- bus
- train

Picture dictionary

Jellybean awards this certificate to

_____

(NAME)

for completing

Jelly beans 3

CONGRATULATIONS!

Jelly beans 3

Rebecca Williams & Katy Smith

Activity Book

Draw, paint, glue and cut.

Jellybeans 3 — Unit 1 **I can do it** Lesson 1

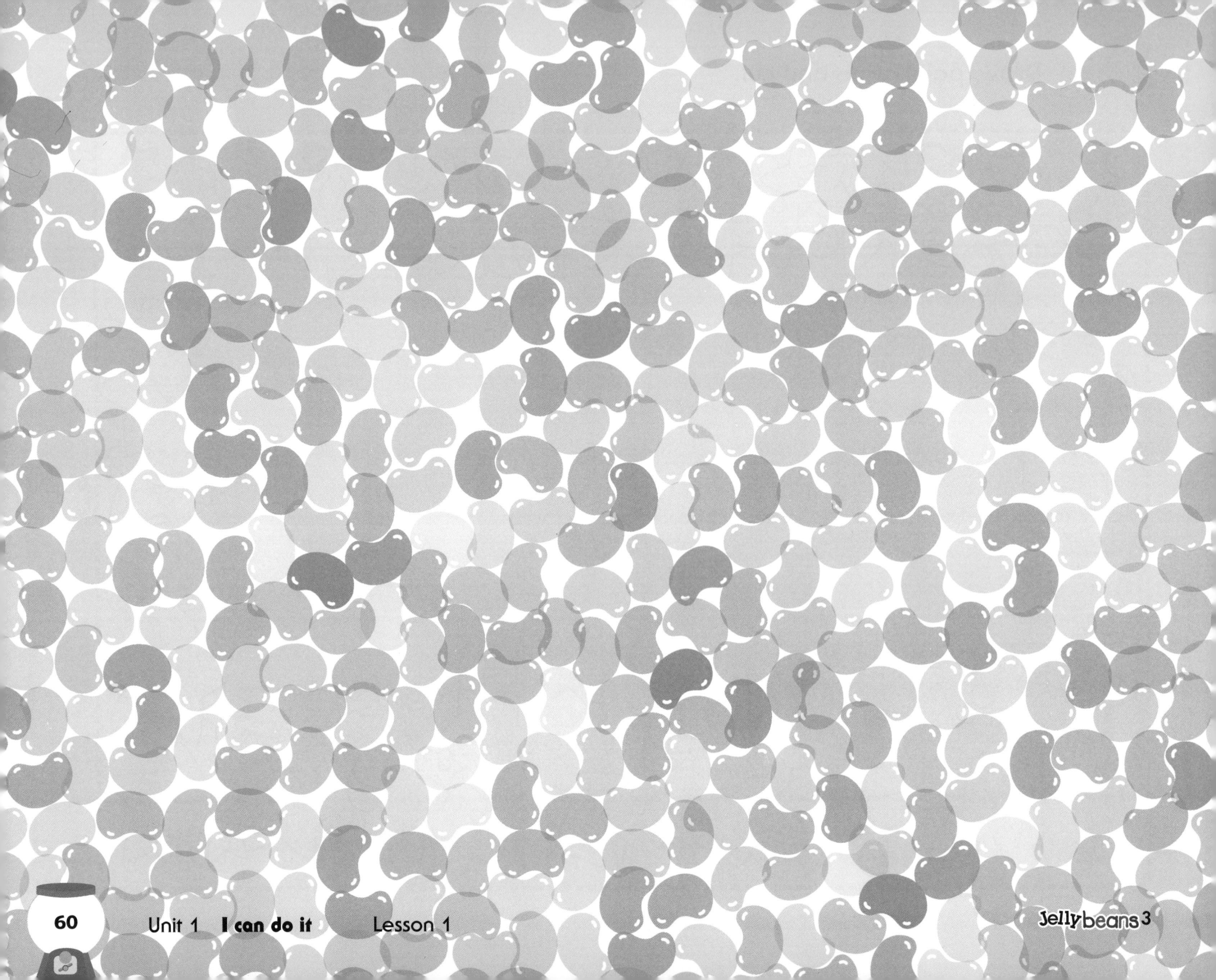

Unit 1   **I can do it**   Lesson 1

Paint, color, cut and glue.

I'm 5!

I'm 6!

Jellybeans 3 — Unit 1 **I can do it** Lesson 1

62　Unit 1　**I can do it**　Lesson 1

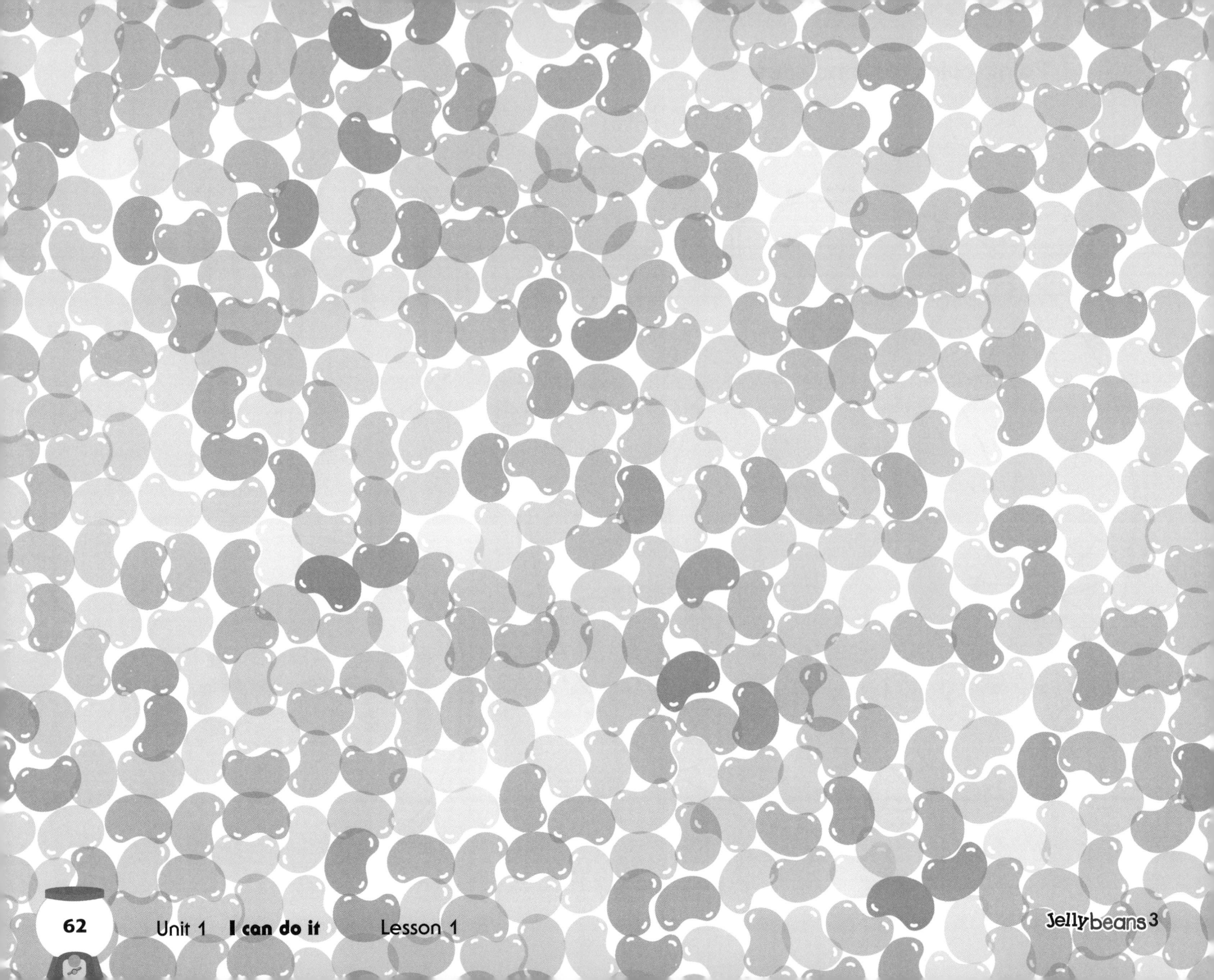

Color, cut and assemble.

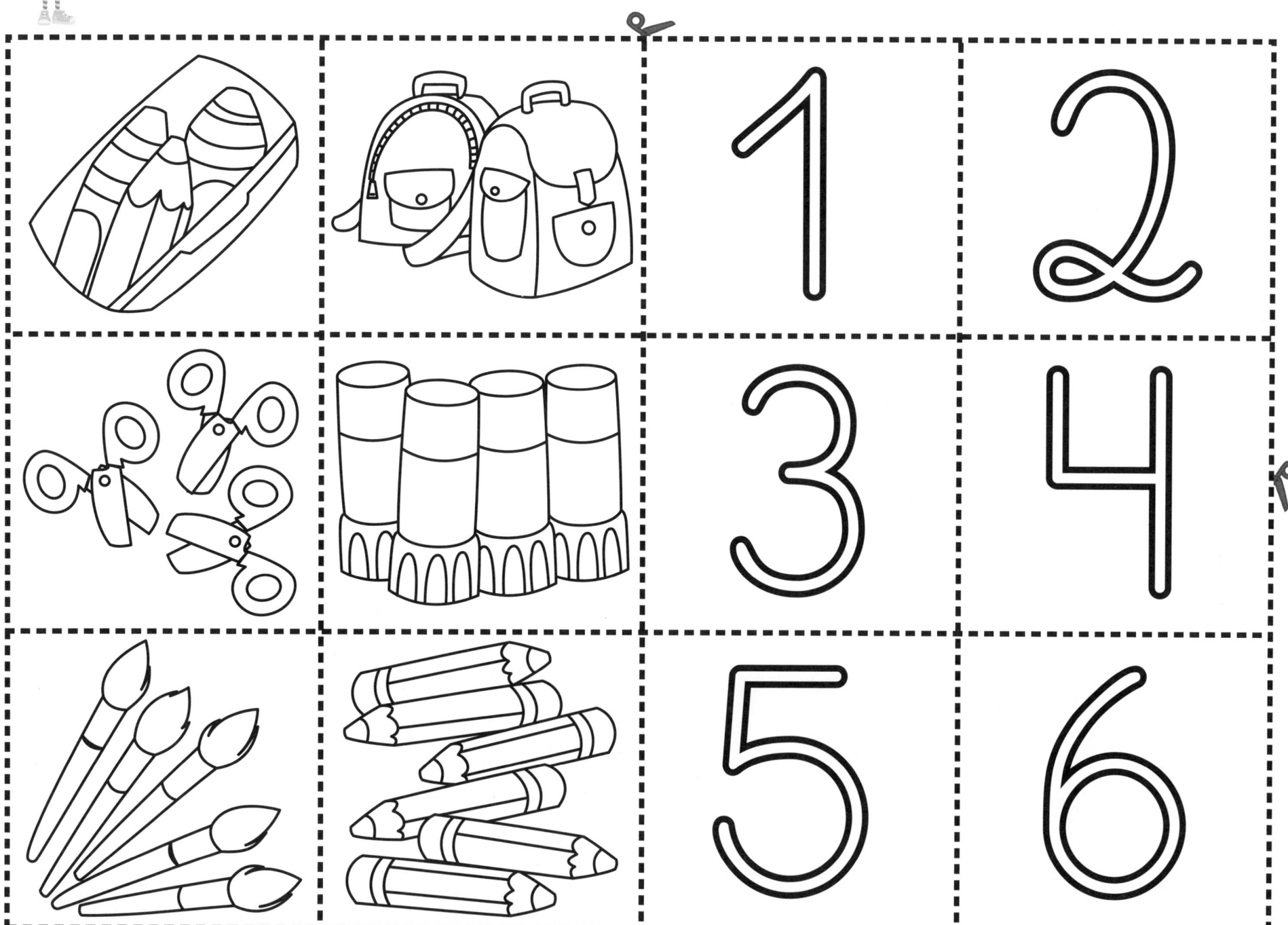

		1	2
		3	4
		5	6

Unit 1 **I can do it** Lesson 2

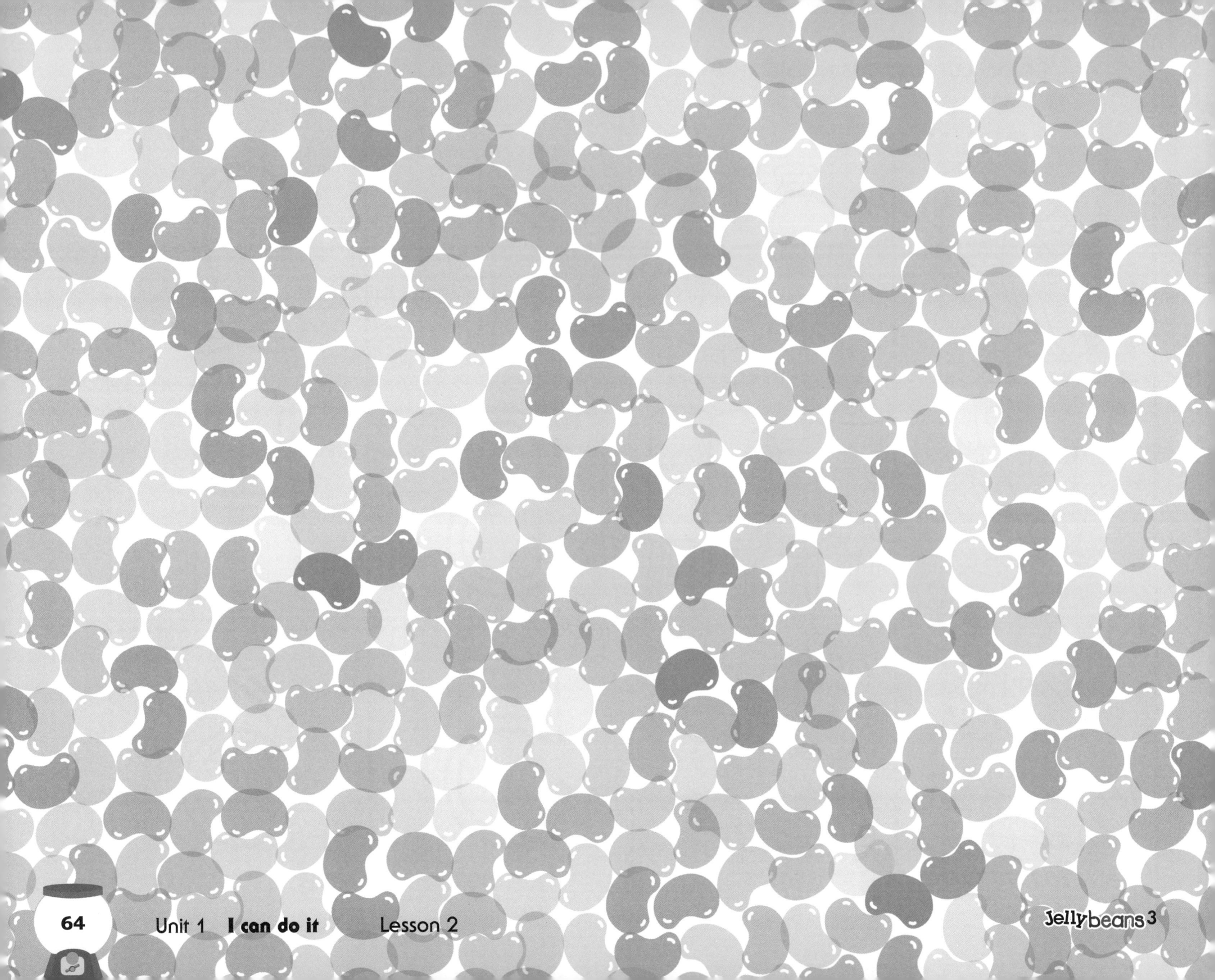

64 Unit 1 I can do it Lesson 2

Color, draw, cut and assemble.

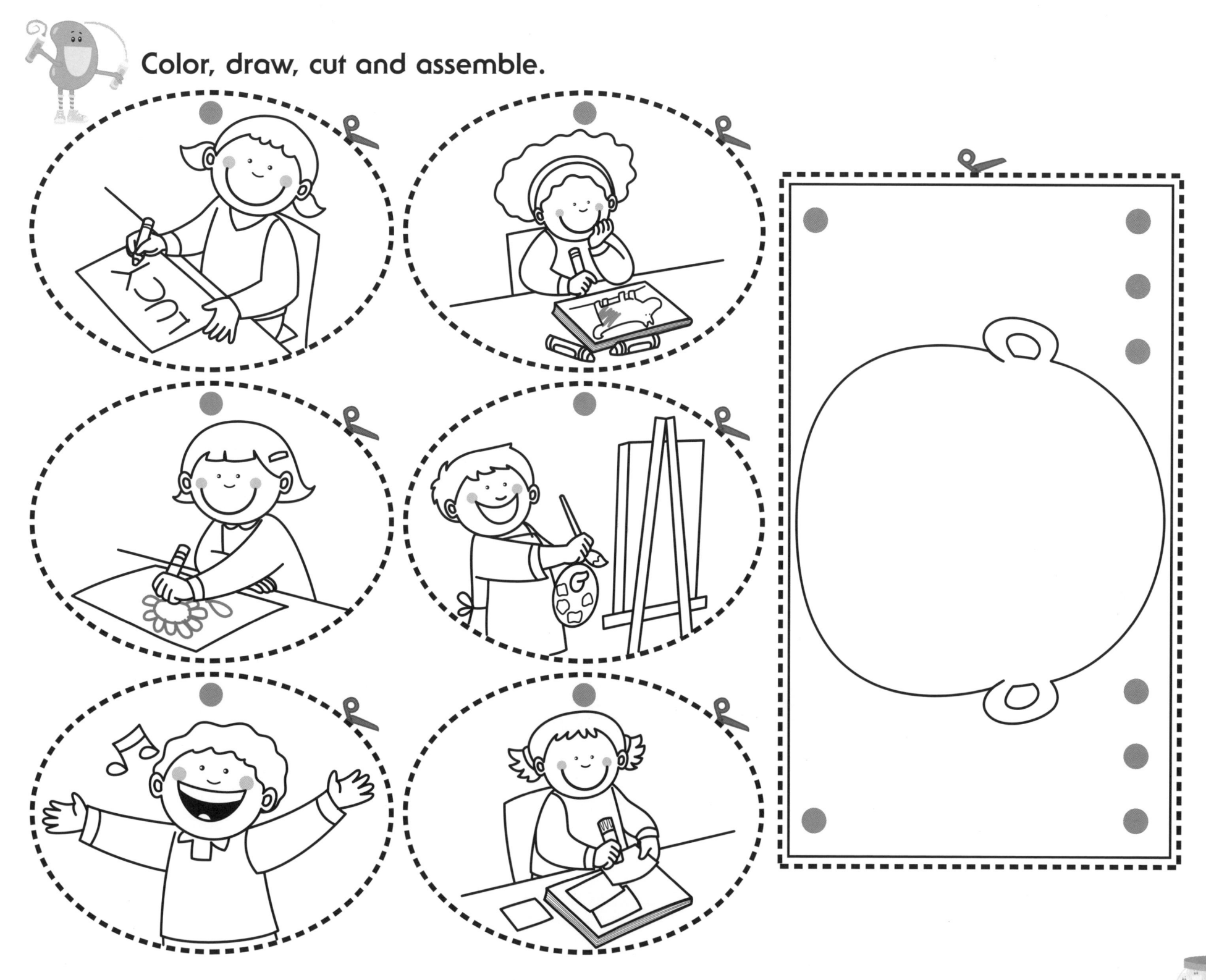

Jellybeans 3

Unit 1 **I can do it** Lesson 2

66 Unit 1 **I can do it** Lesson 2

Cut, paint, glue and assemble.

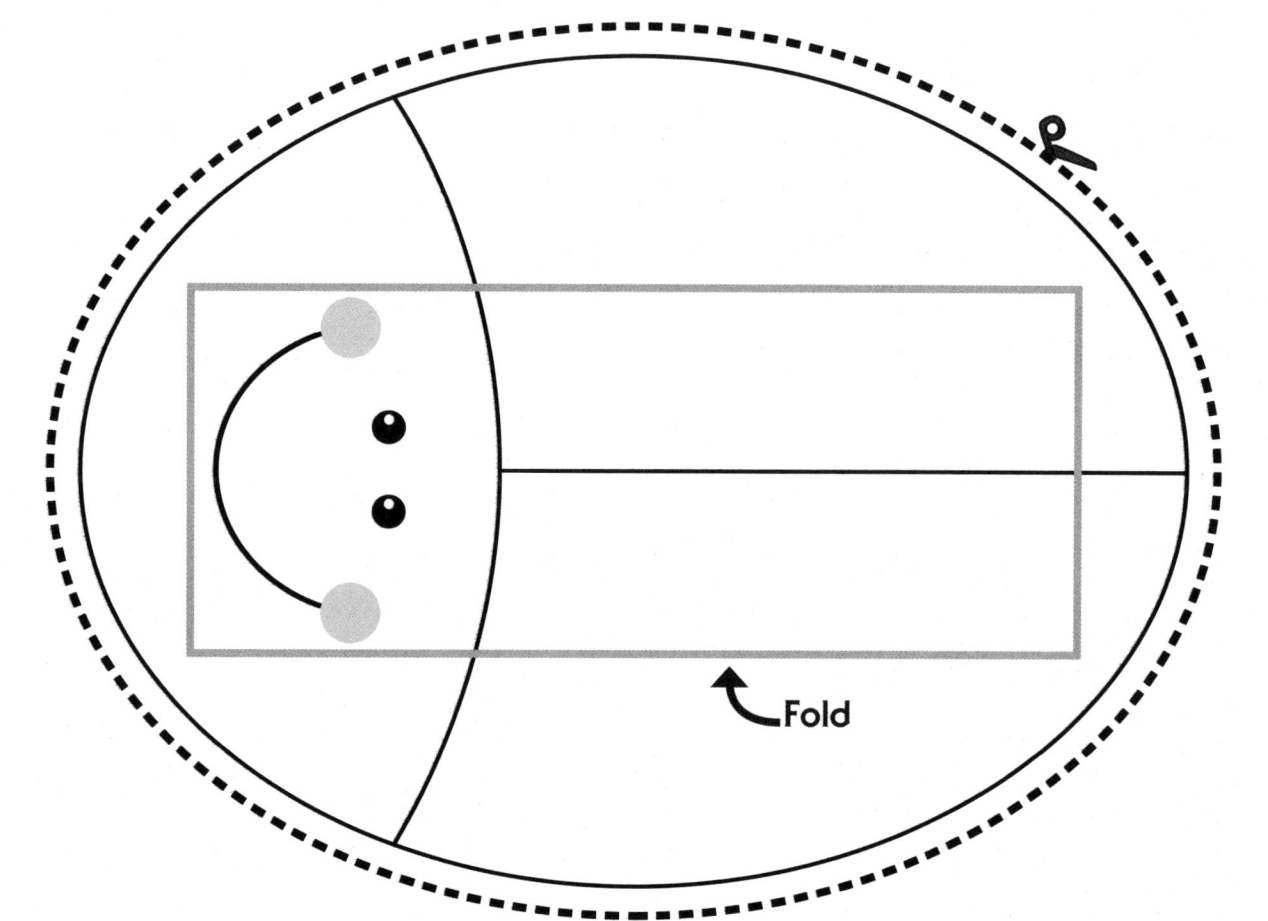

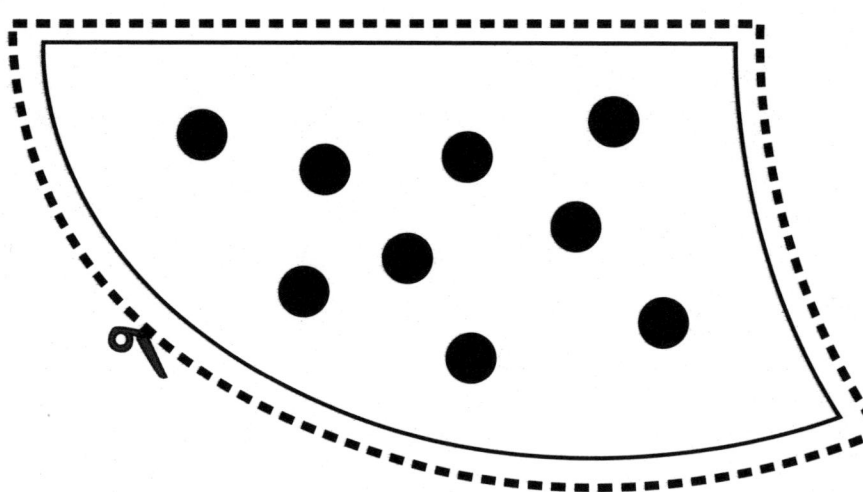

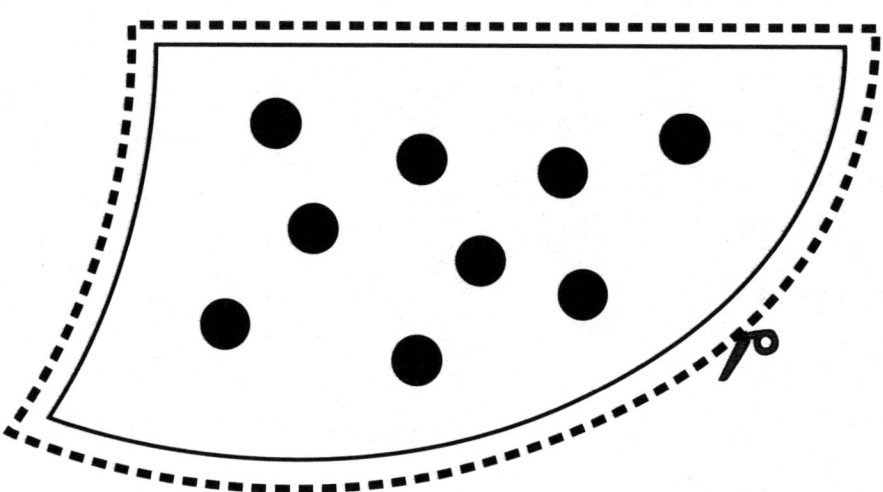

Fold

Jellybeans 3 Unit 2 **One bug, two bugs** Lesson 1 67

Unit 2 **One bug, two bugs** Lesson 1

Color, paint and cut.

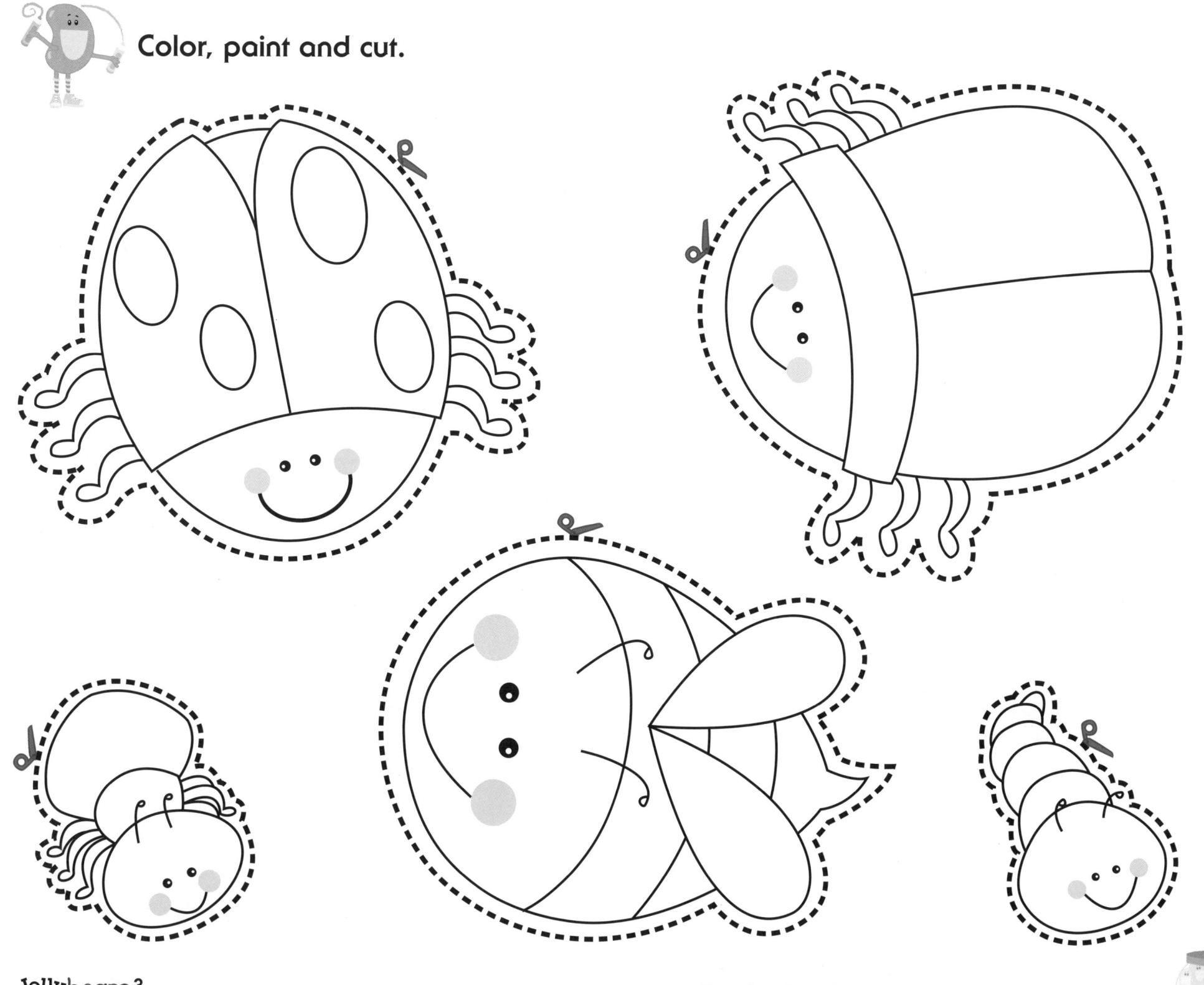

Jellybeans 3

Unit 2 **One bug, two bugs** Lesson 1

69

70 Unit 2 **One bug, two bugs** Lesson 1 Jellybeans 3

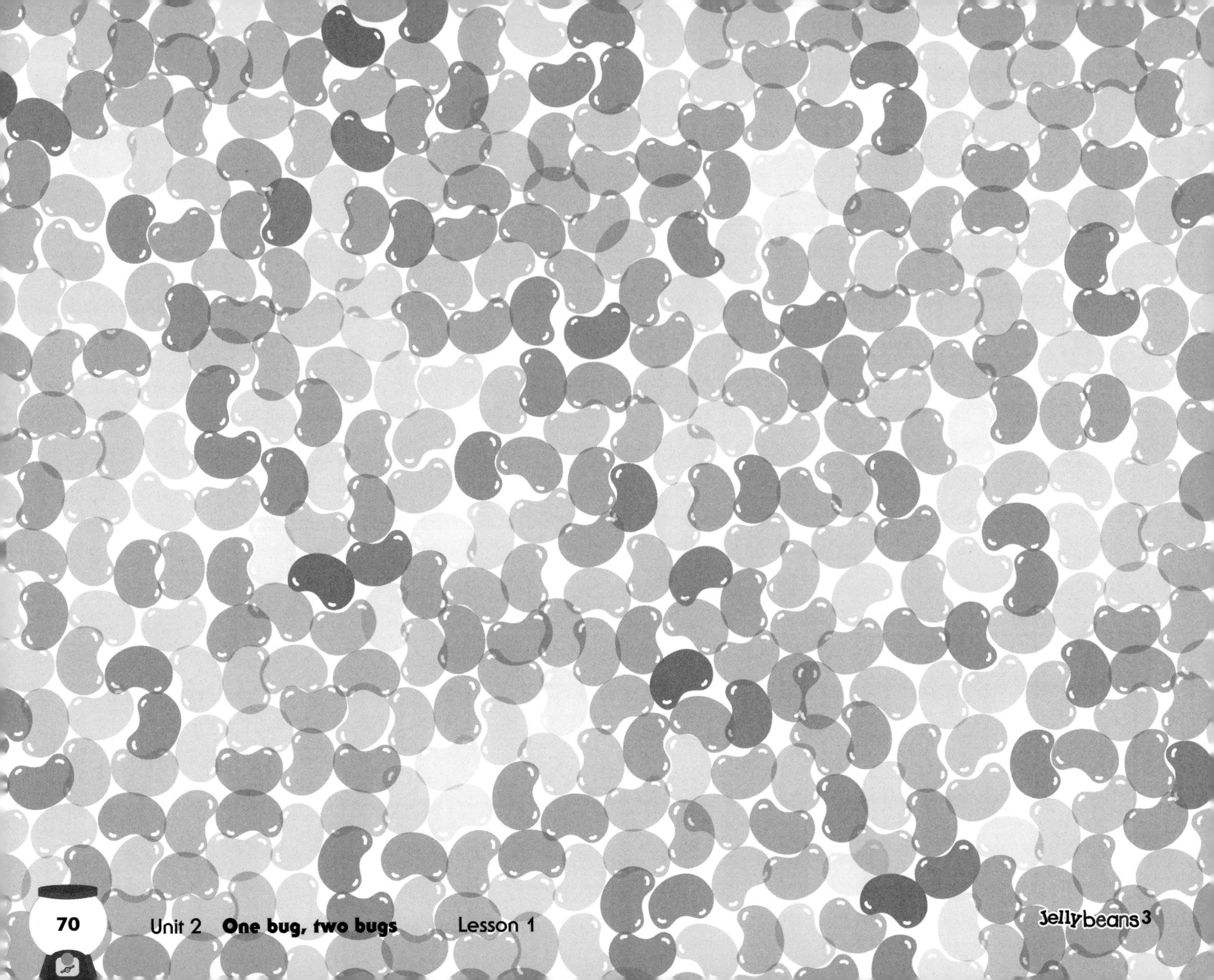

Color, cut and play *Concentration*.

Jellybeans 3   Unit 2 **One bug, two bugs**   Lesson 2   71

Color, cut and glue.

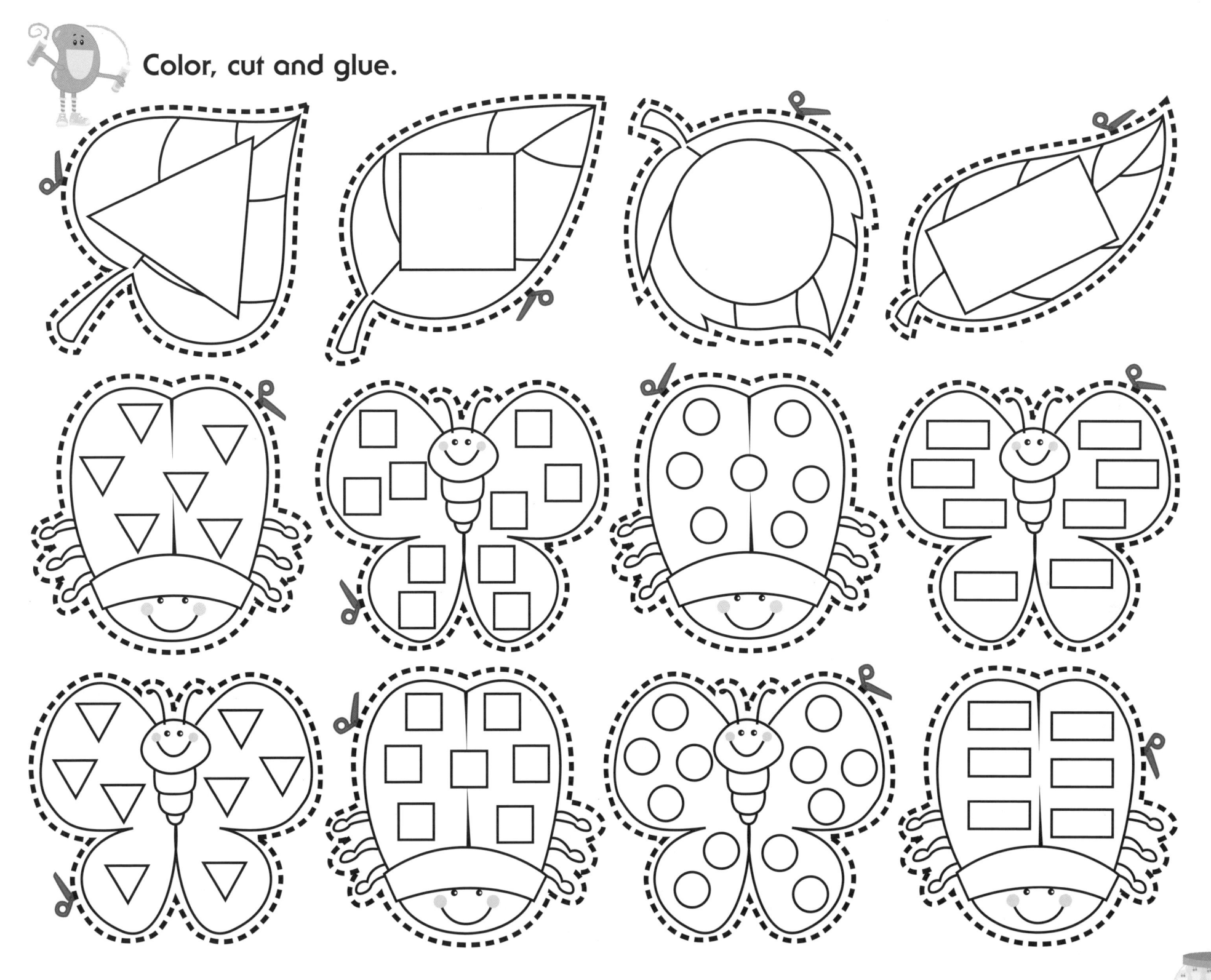

Jellybeans 3

Unit 2 **One bug, two bugs** Lesson 2

73

74 Unit 2 **One bug, two bugs** Lesson 2 Jellybeans 3

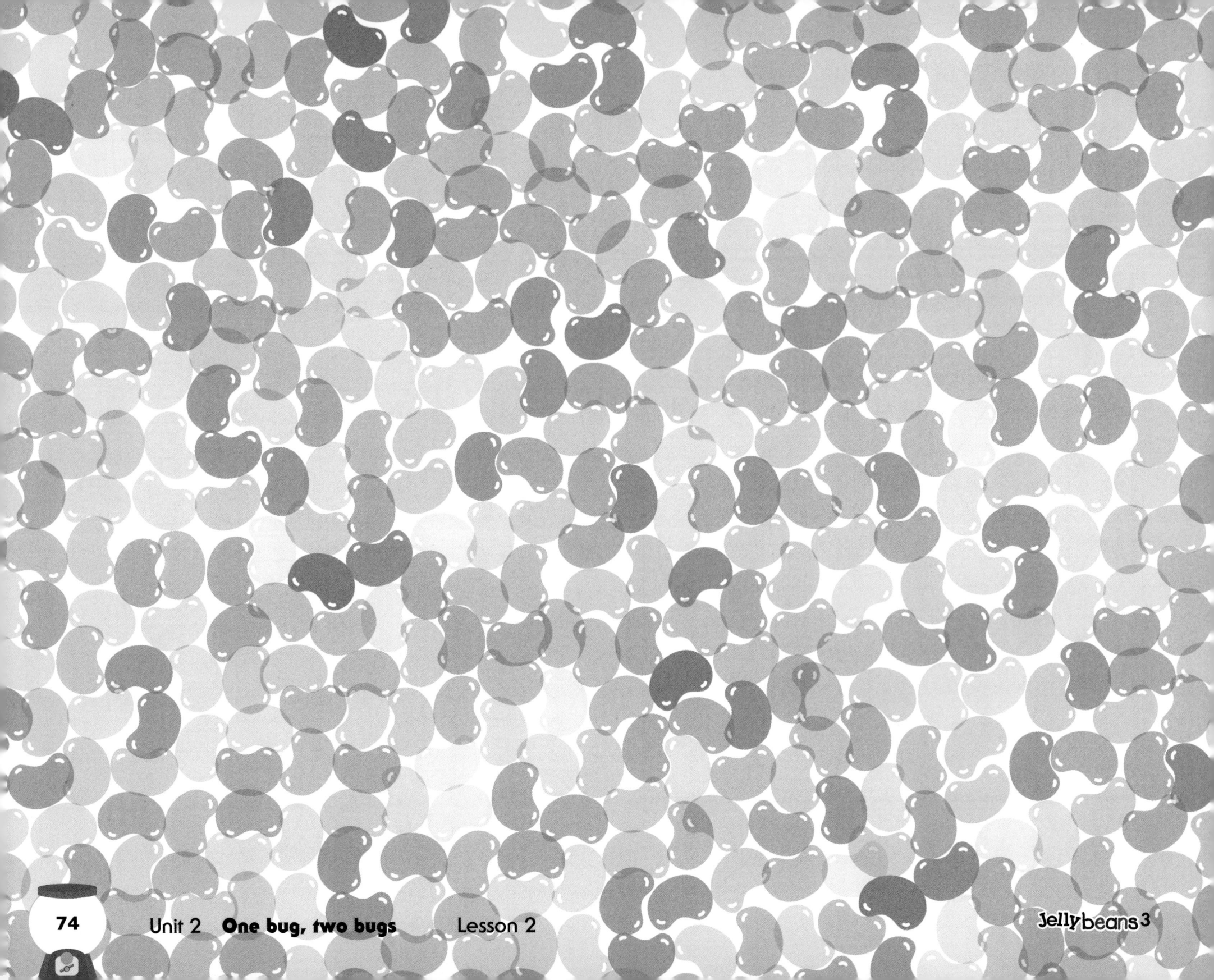

Color, cut and assemble.

Jellybeans 3

Unit 3   **My healthy body**   Lesson 1

75

Unit 3 **My healthy body** Lesson 1

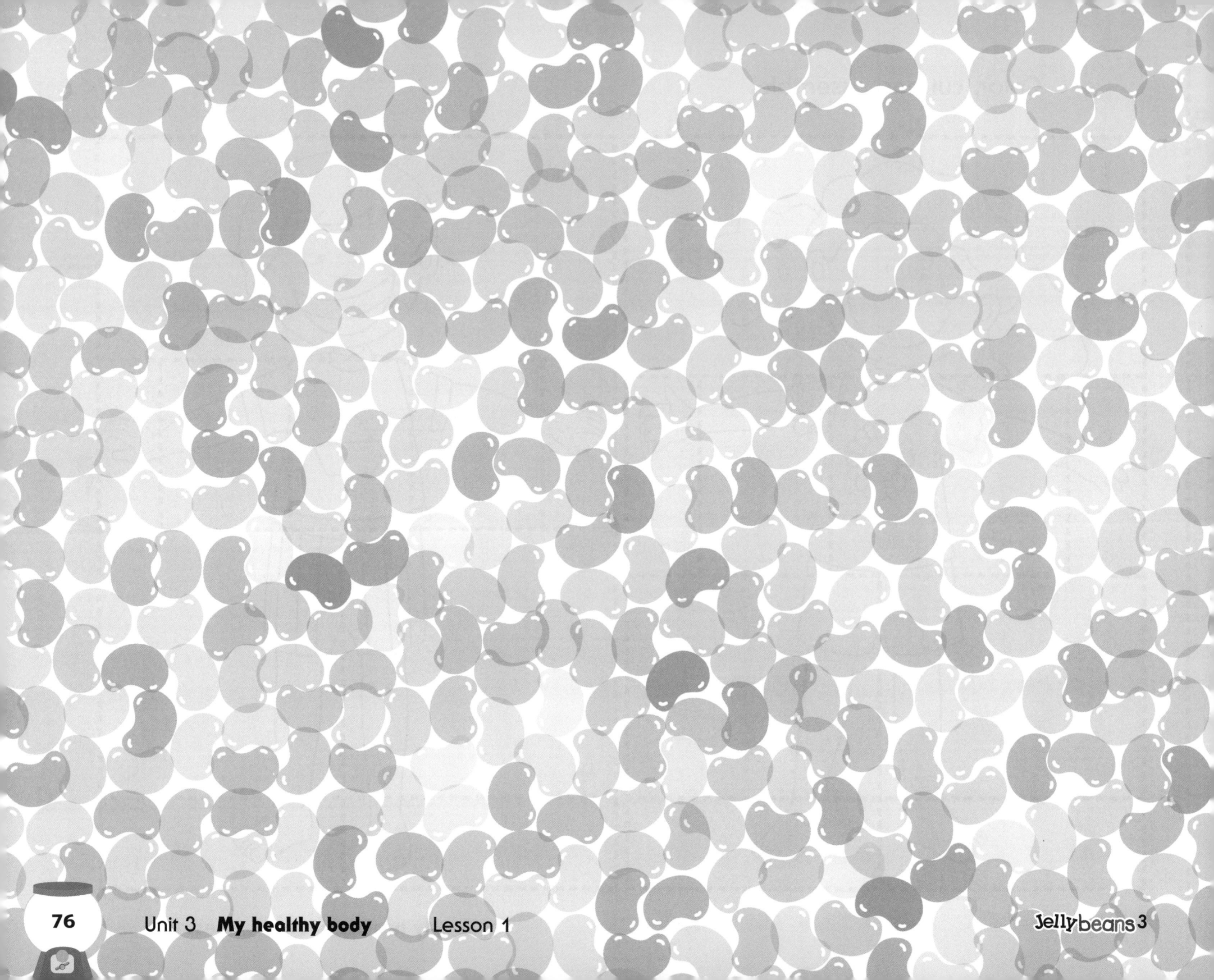

Color, cut and assemble.

Unit 3 **My healthy body** Lesson 1

78 Unit 3 **My healthy body** Lesson 1

Jellybeans 3

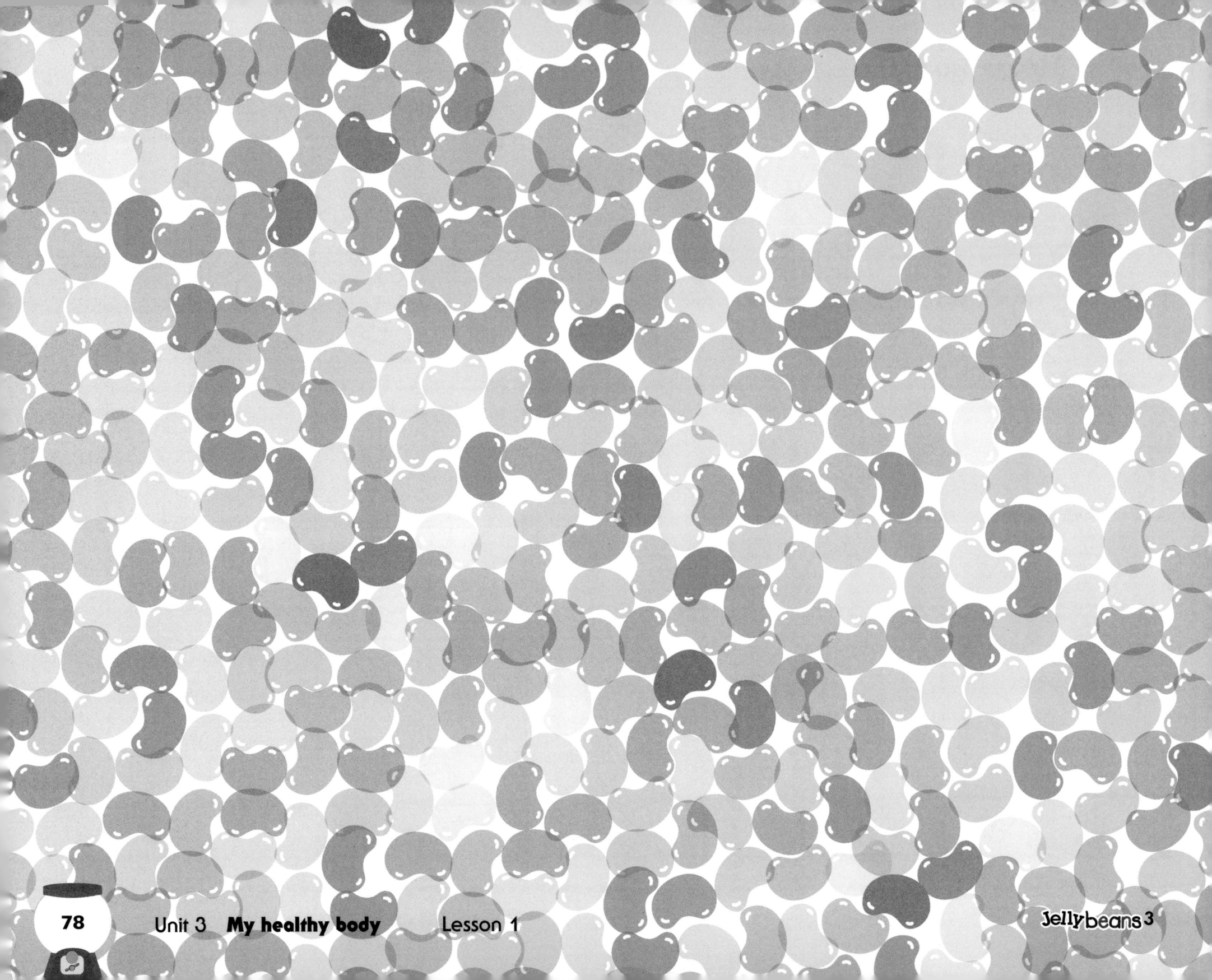

Finger-paint and cut.

Jellybeans 3

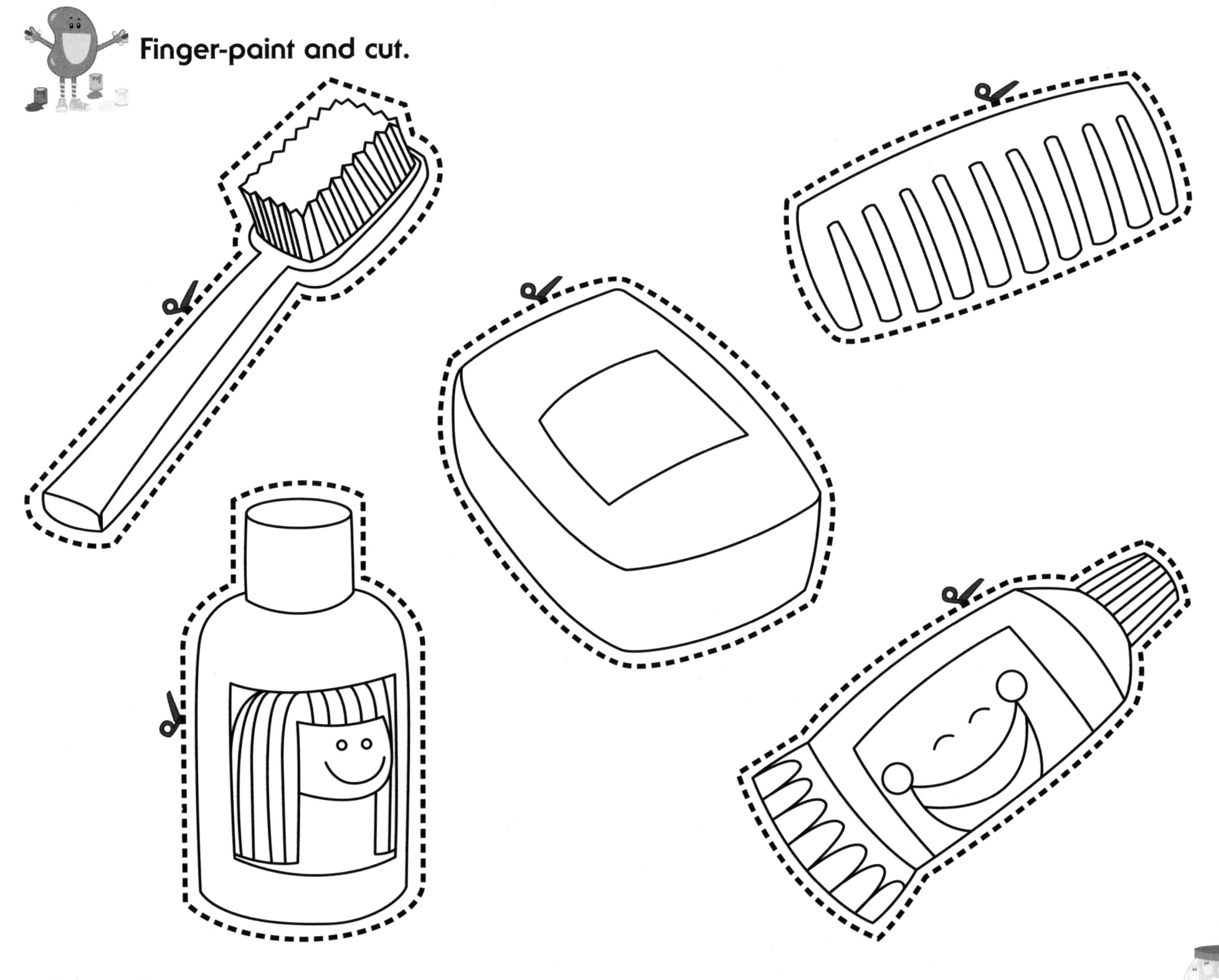

Unit 3 **My healthy body** Lesson 2

79

80 Unit 3 **My healthy body** Lesson 2

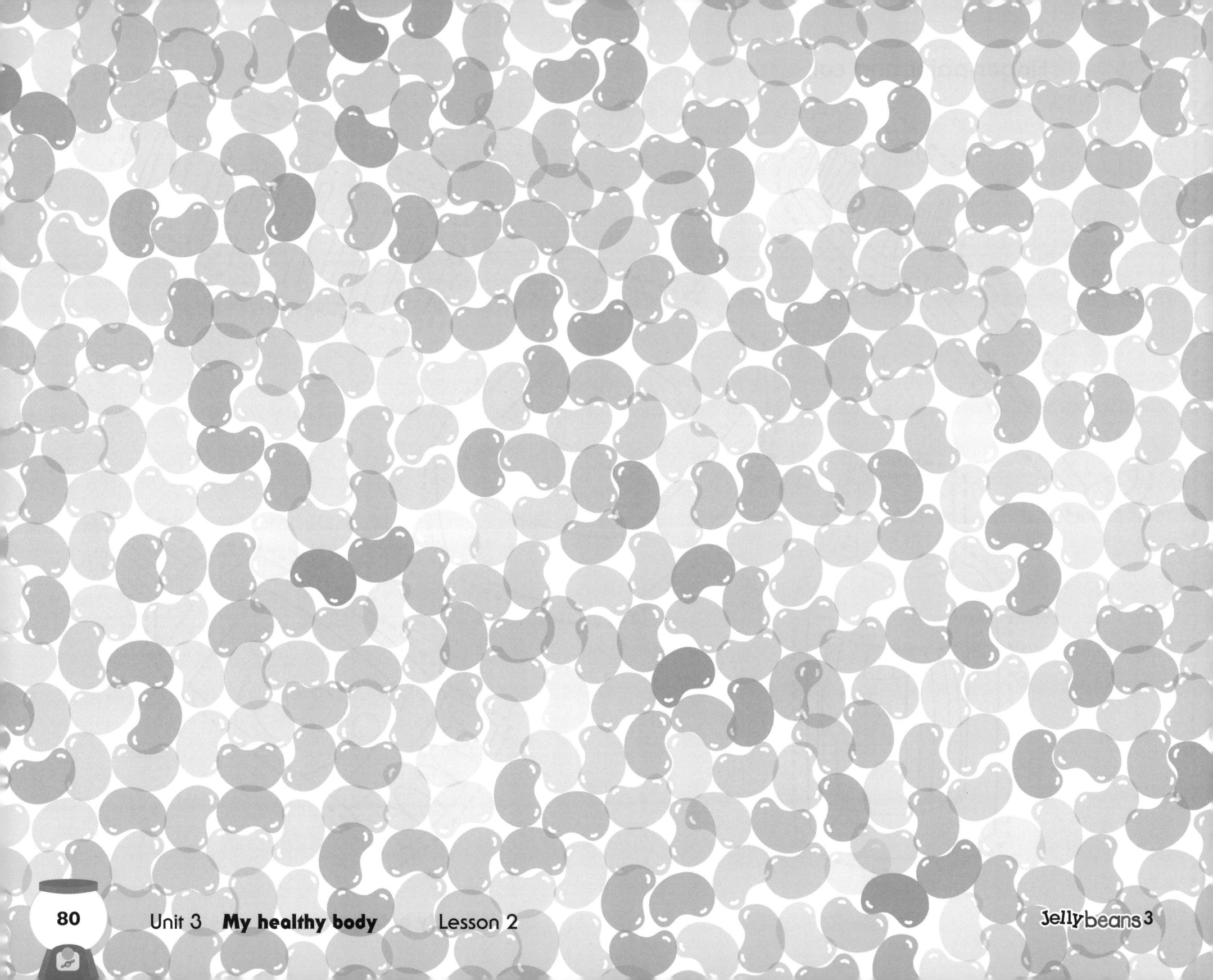

Finger-paint, cut and assemble.

Jellybeans 3

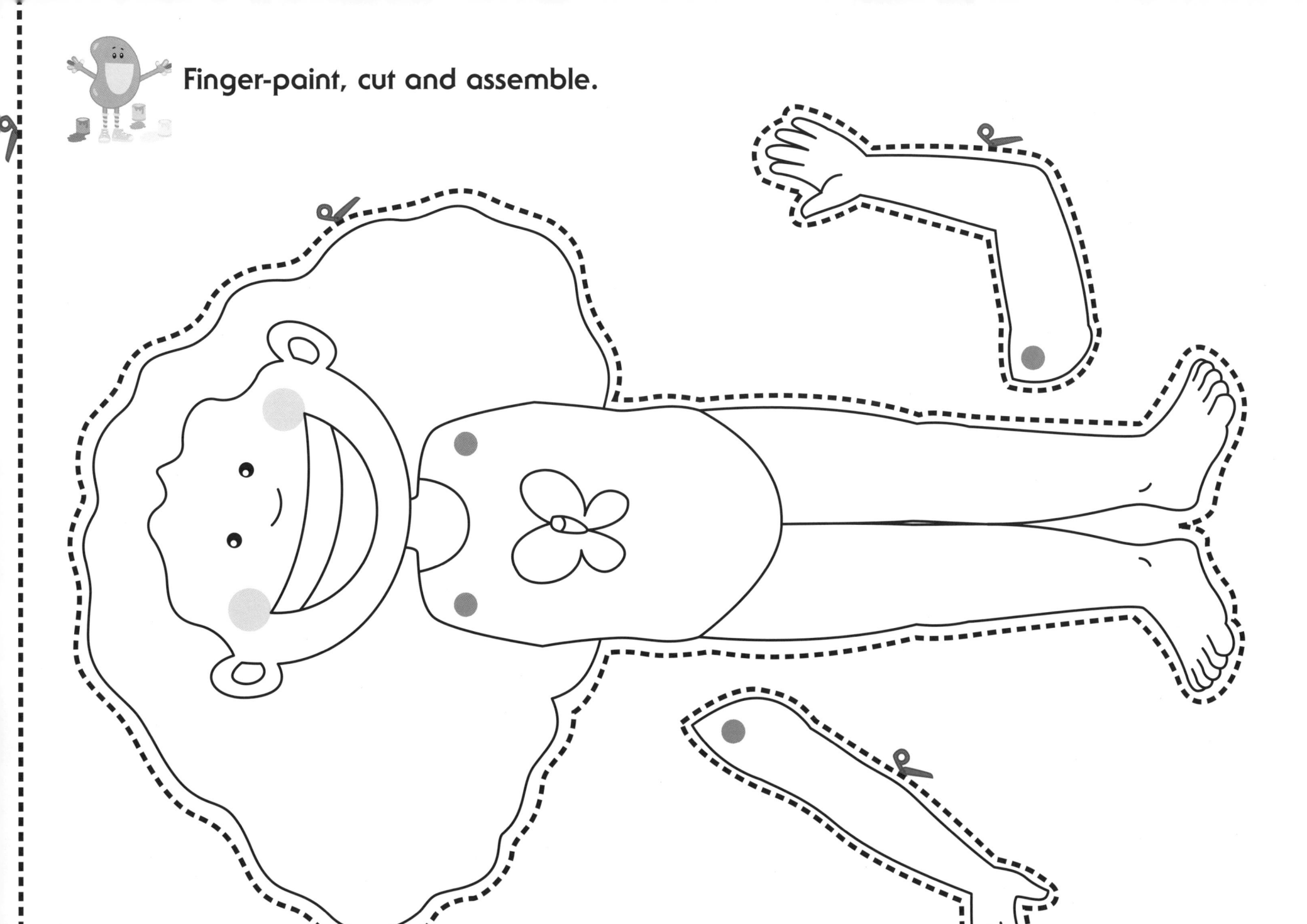

Unit 3 **My healthy body** Lesson 2

81

Unit 3 **My healthy body** Lesson 2

Look, color and paint.

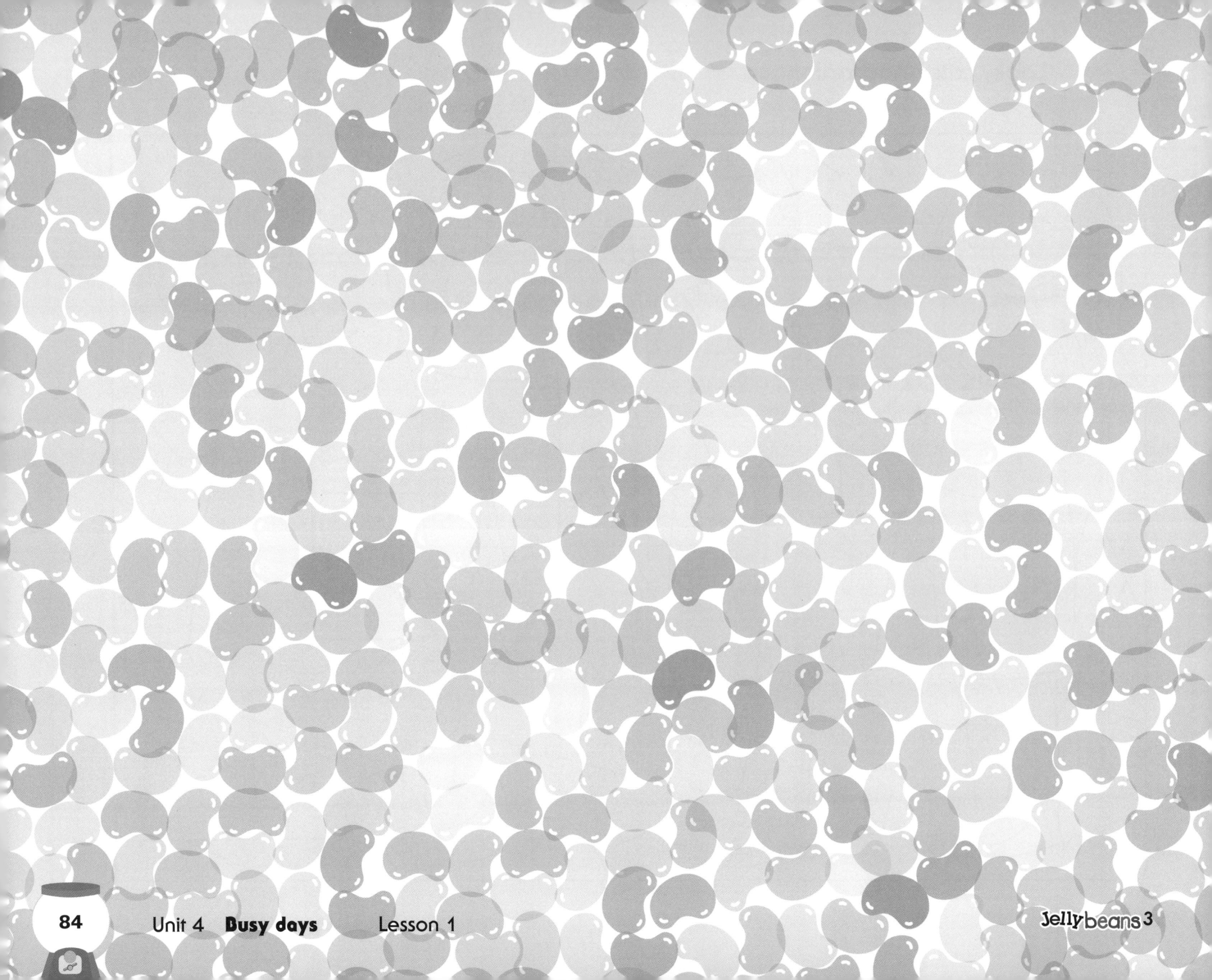

Unit 4 **Busy days** Lesson 1

Color, cut, glue and paint.

Glue

Glue

Glue

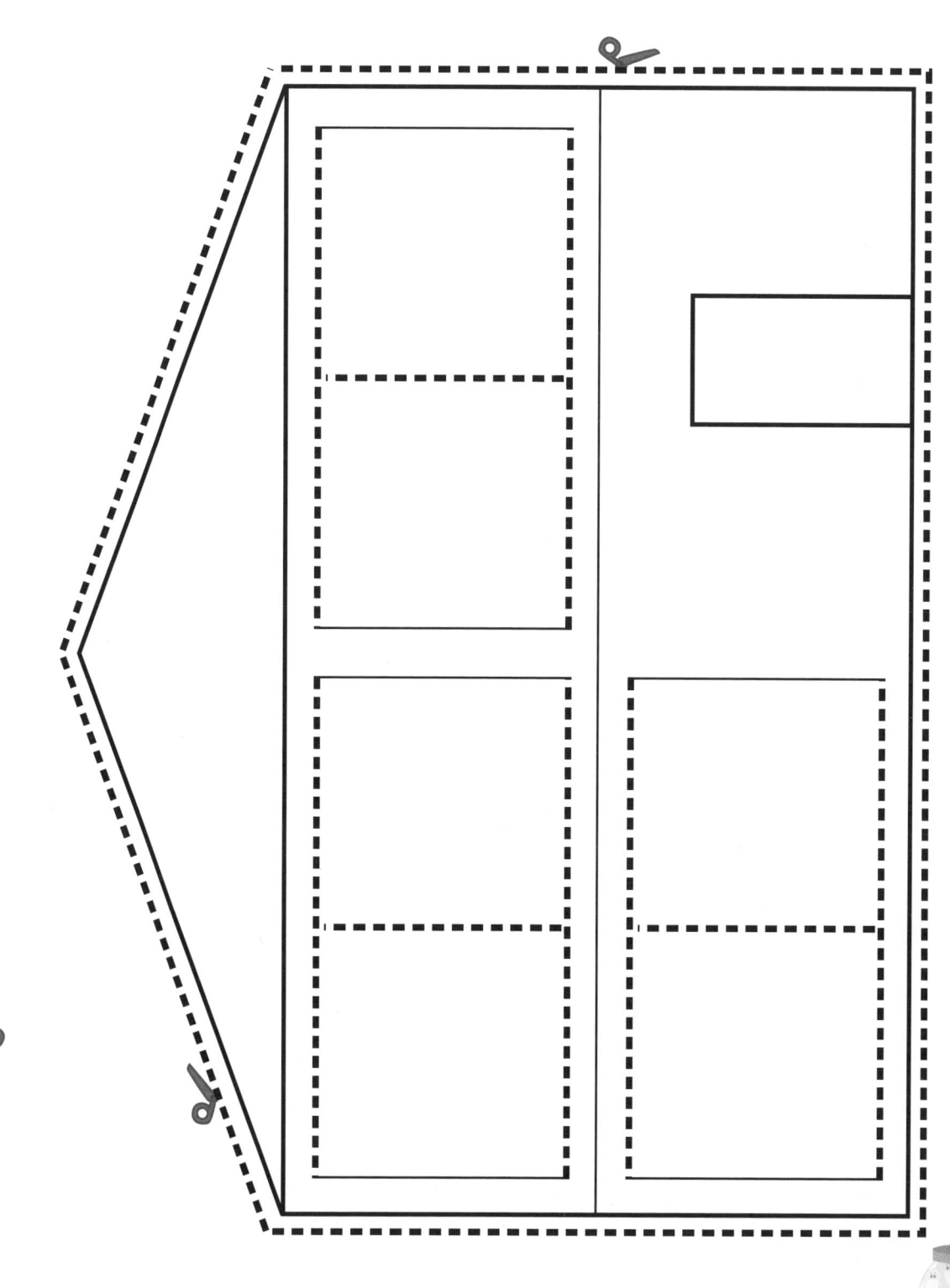

Jellybeans 3

Unit 4 **Busy days** Lesson 1

85

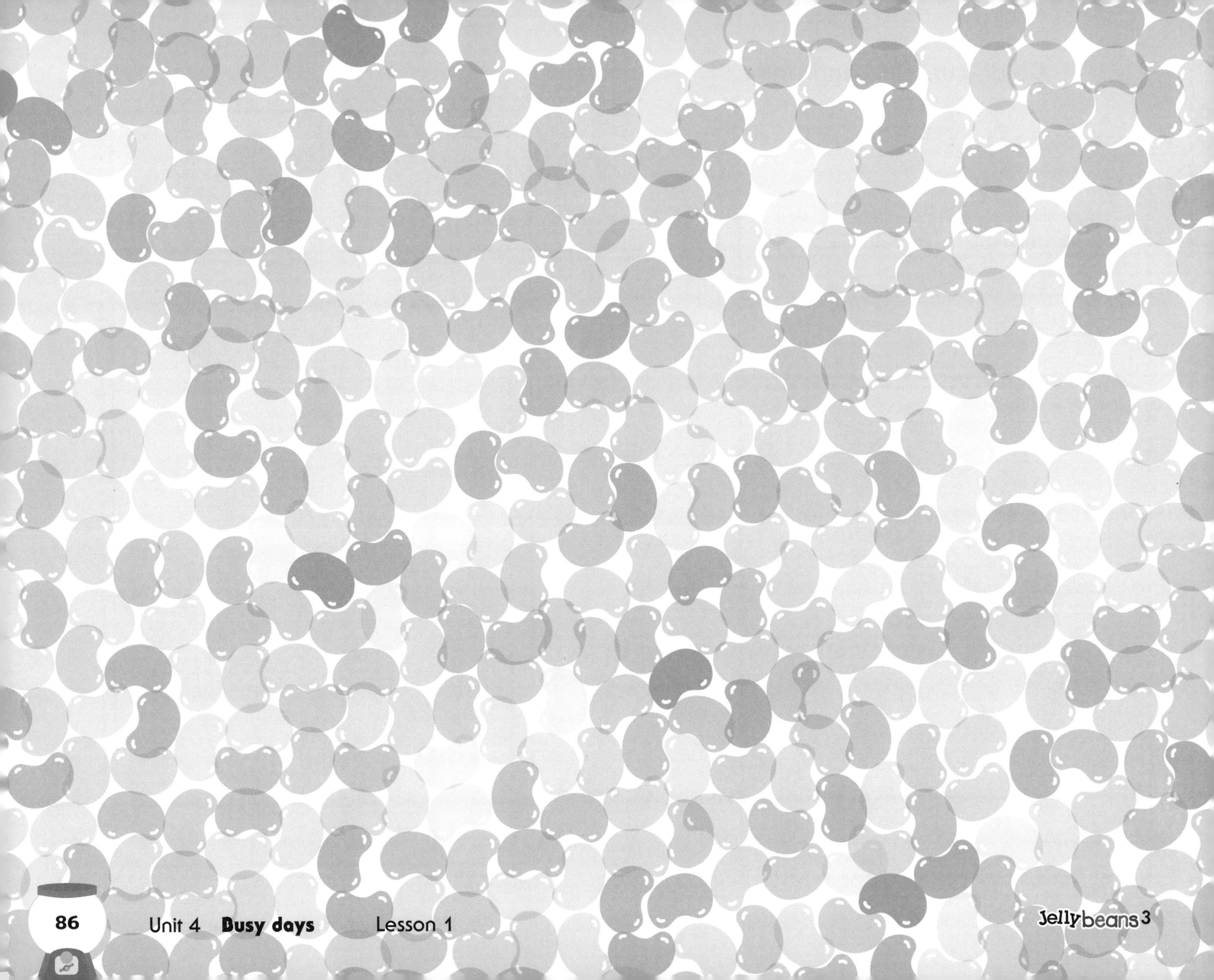

Unit 4 **Busy days** Lesson 1

Color, cut and assemble.

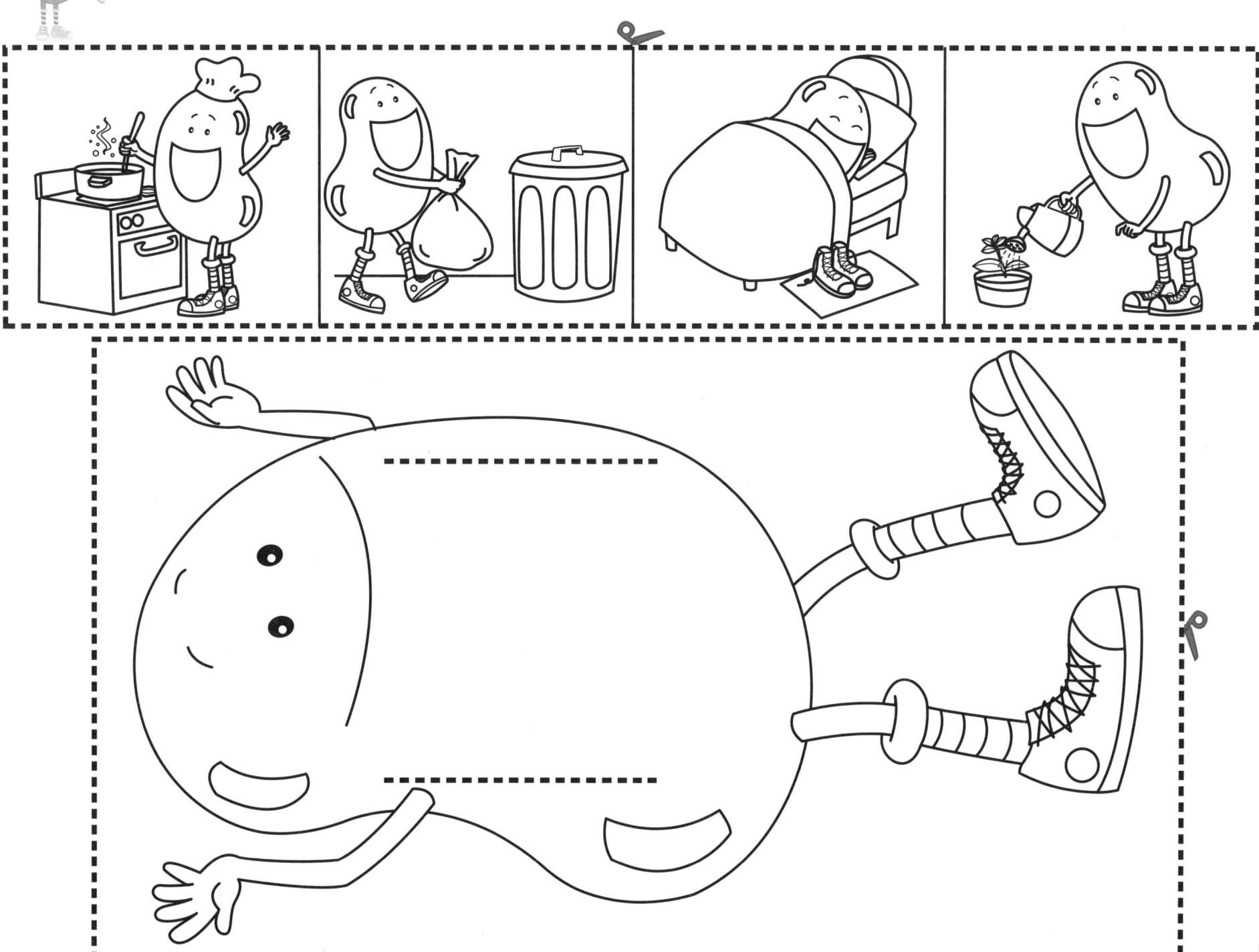

Unit 4 **Busy days** Lesson 2

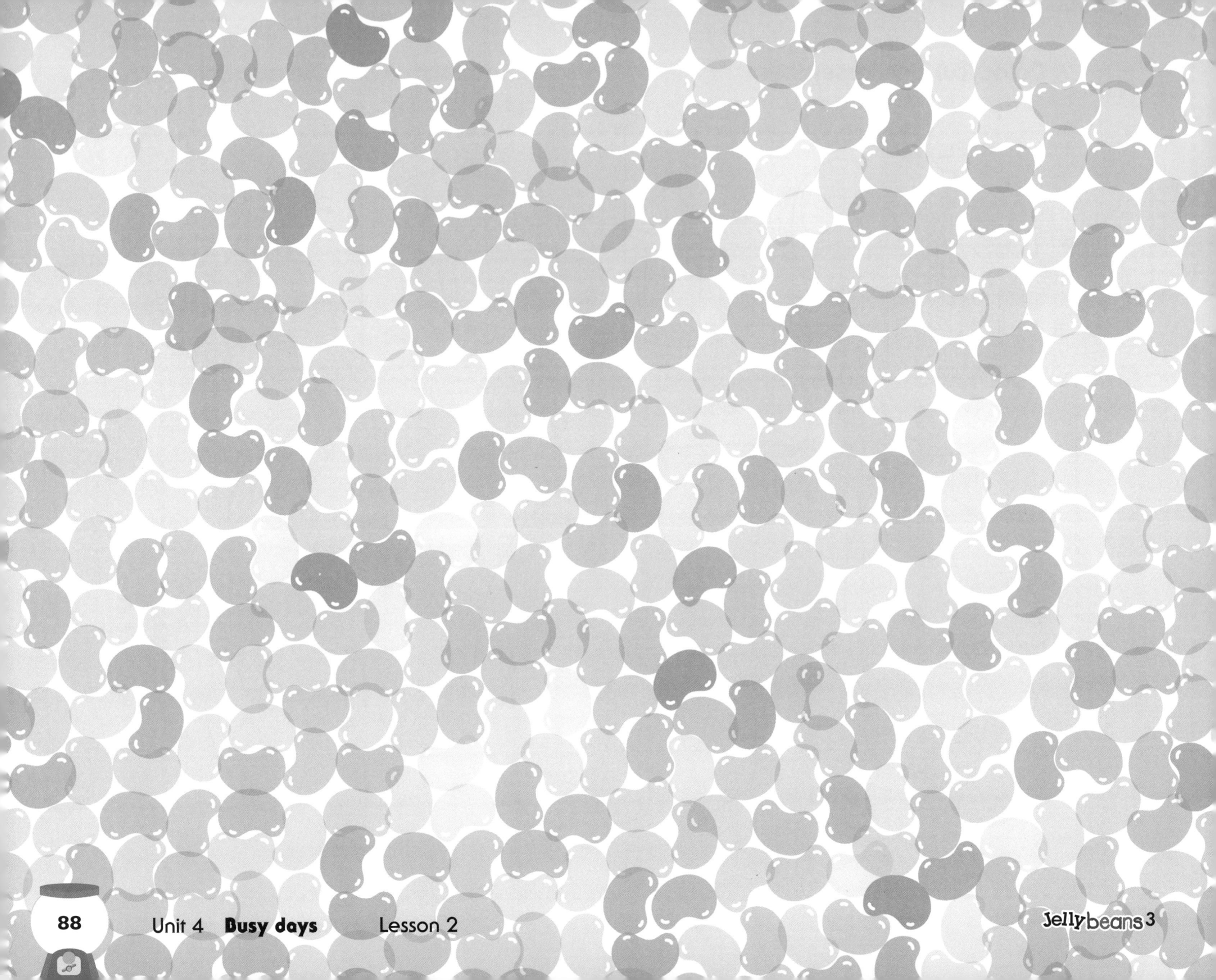

Color, glue, cut and assemble.

I CAN HELP!

Jellybeans 3

Unit 4 **Busy days** Lesson 2

89

Unit 4 **Busy days** Lesson 2

Paint, glue, cut and assemble.

Jellybeans 3 — Unit 5 **My world** Lesson 1

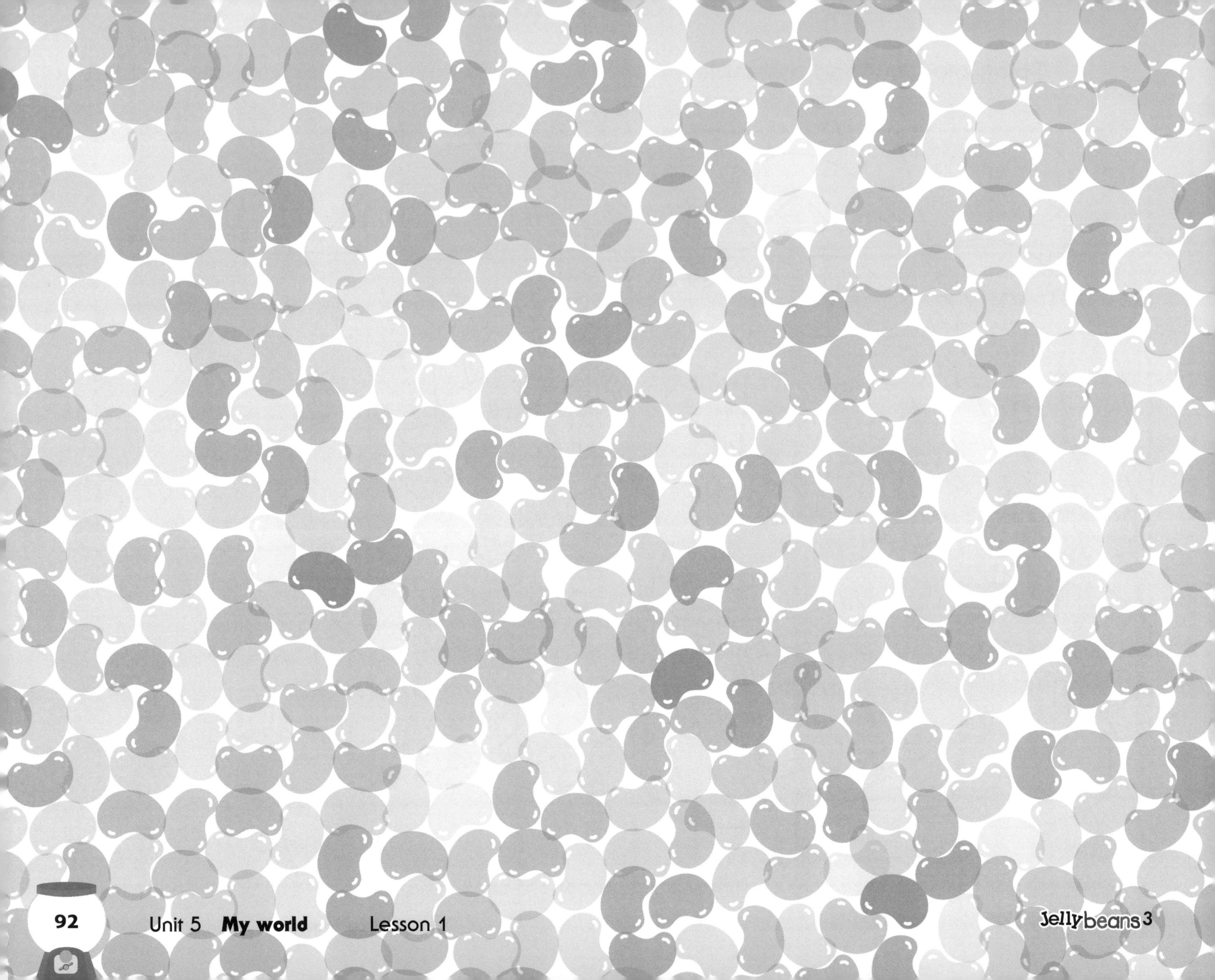

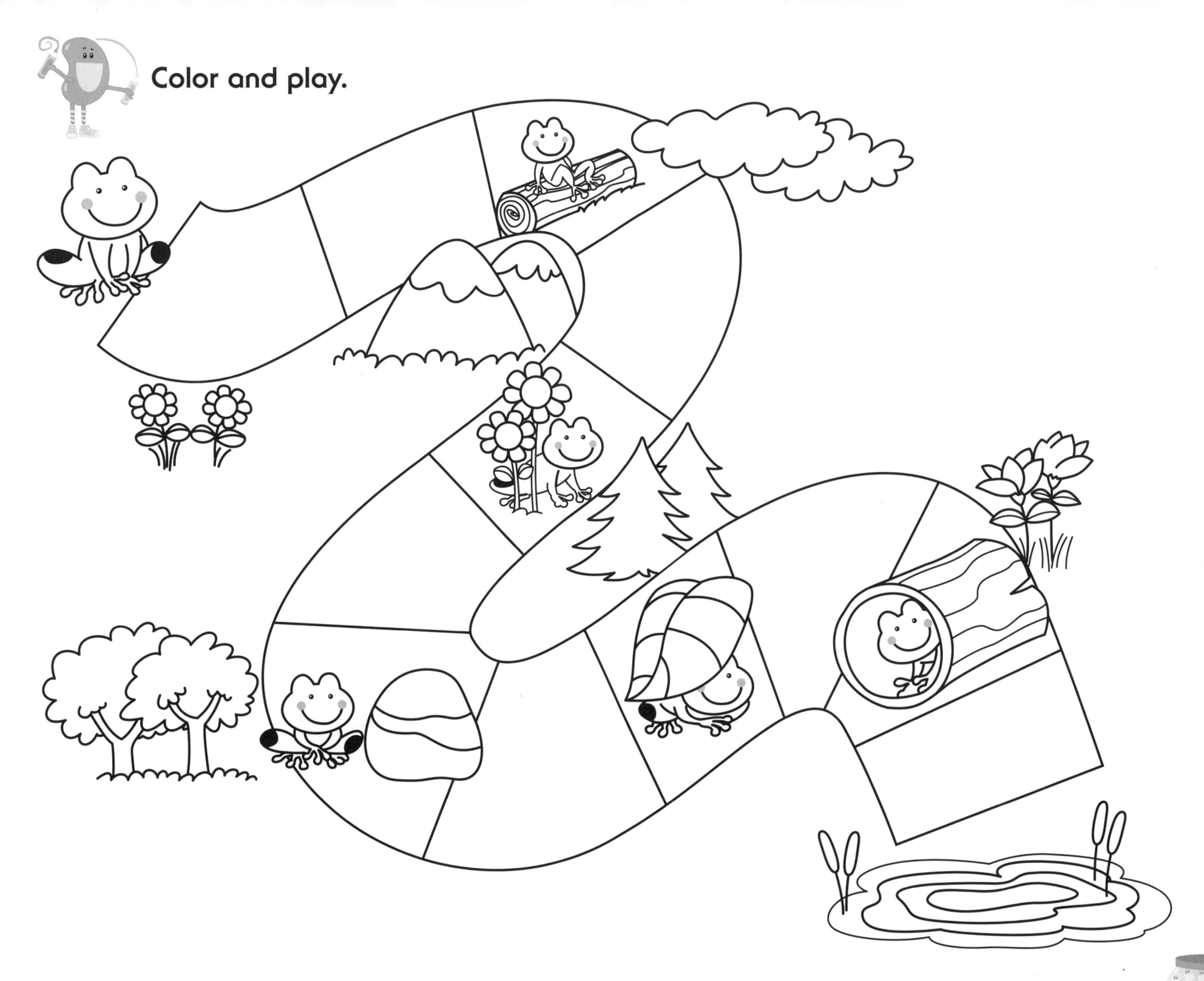

Color and play.

Unit 5 **My world** Lesson 1

94   Unit 5   **My world**   Lesson 1

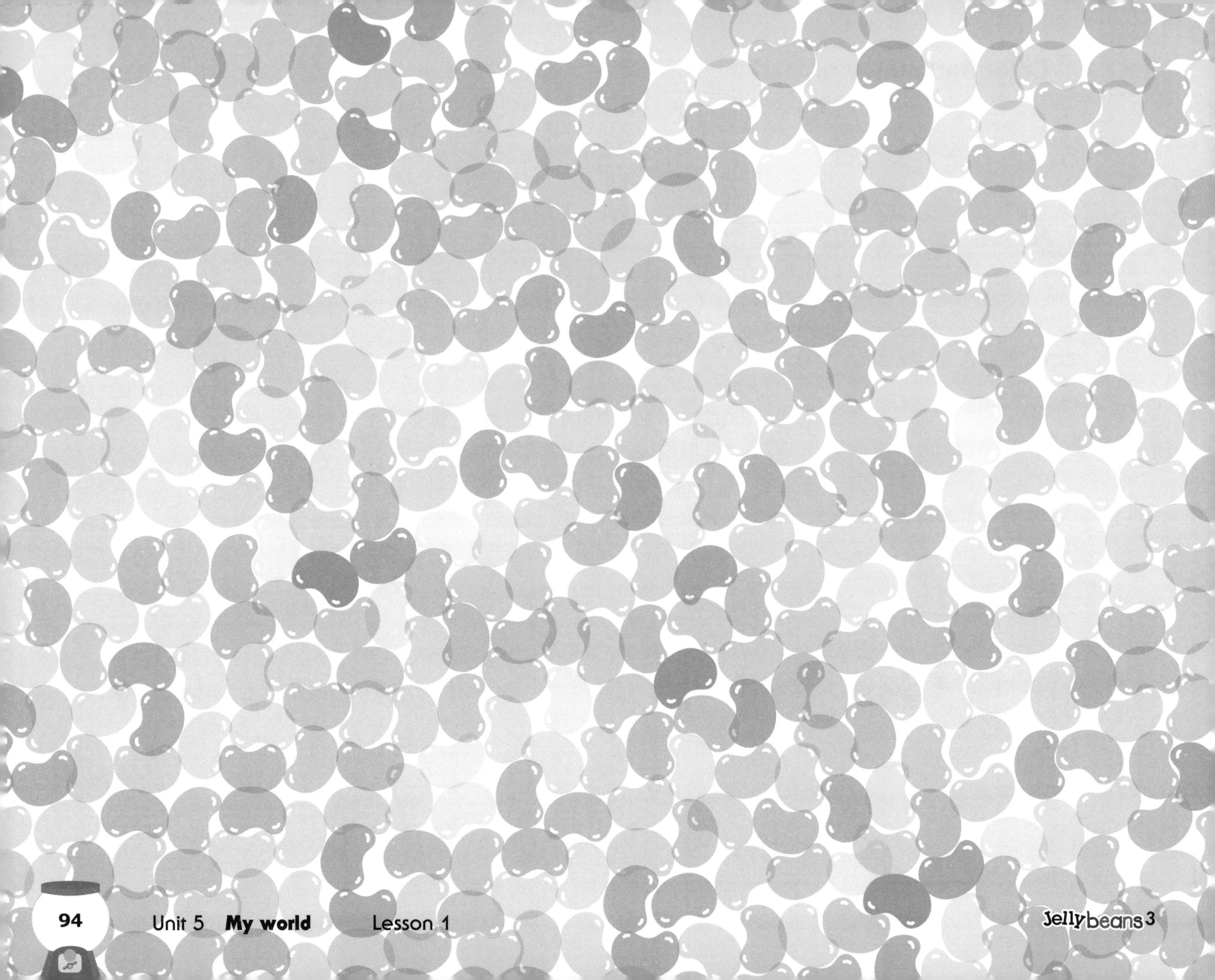

Color, cut and glue.

Fold

Fold

Fold

Fold

Fold

Jellybeans 3

Unit 5 **My world** Lesson 2

95

96 Unit 5 **My world** Lesson 2

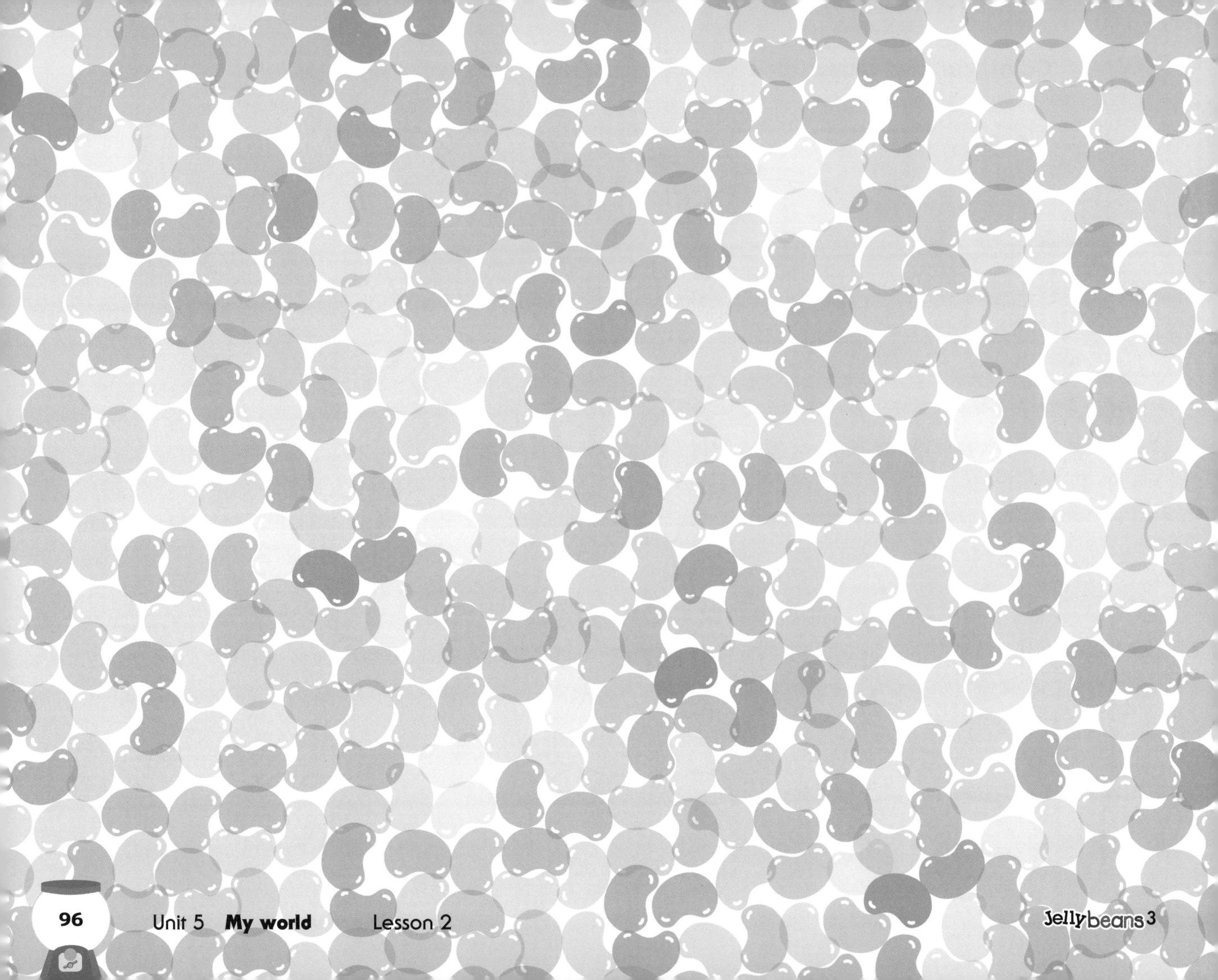

Jellybeans 3

Paint, cut and assemble.

Fold

Jellybeans 3

Unit 5　**My world**　Lesson 2

97

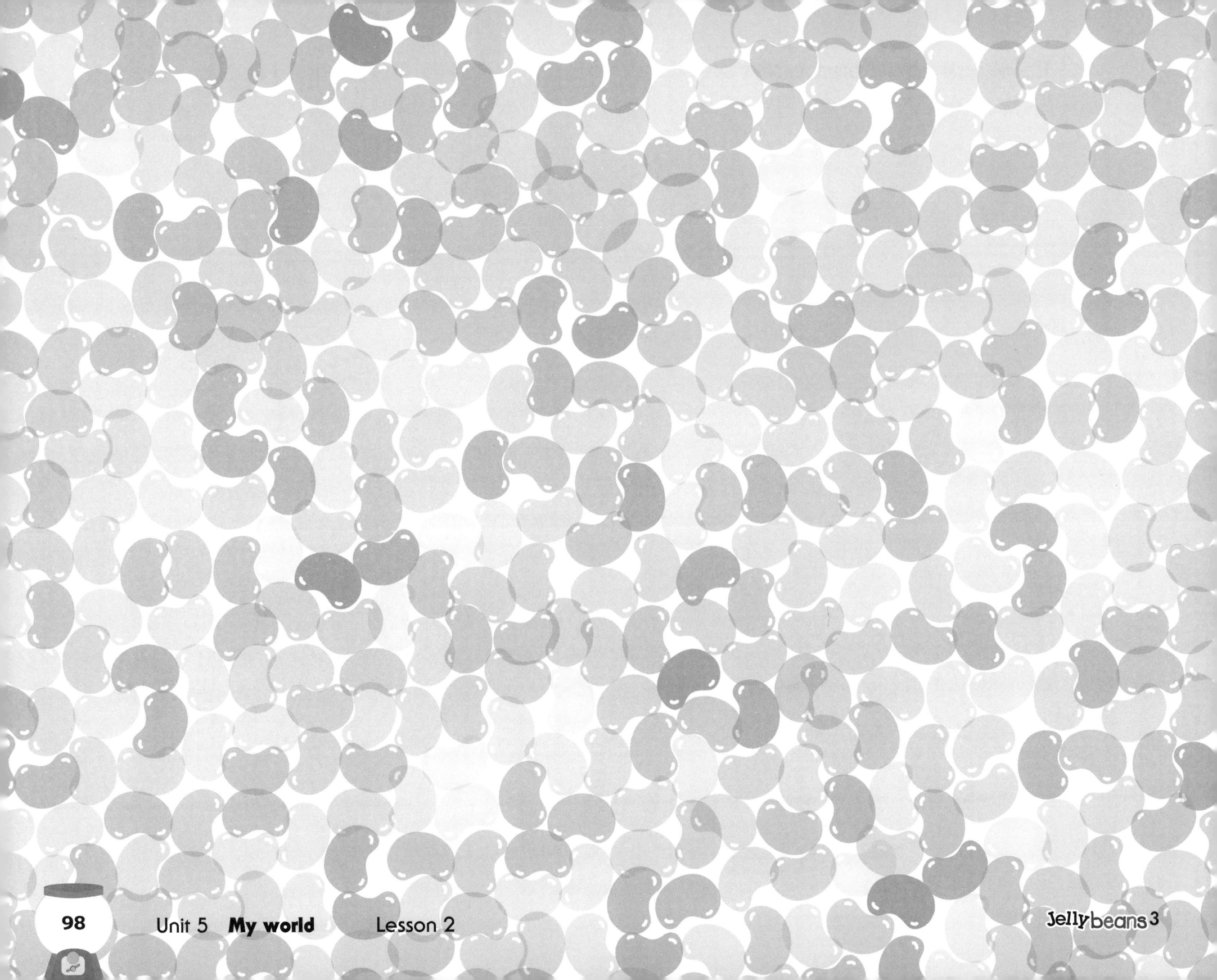

Color, cut, glue and assemble.

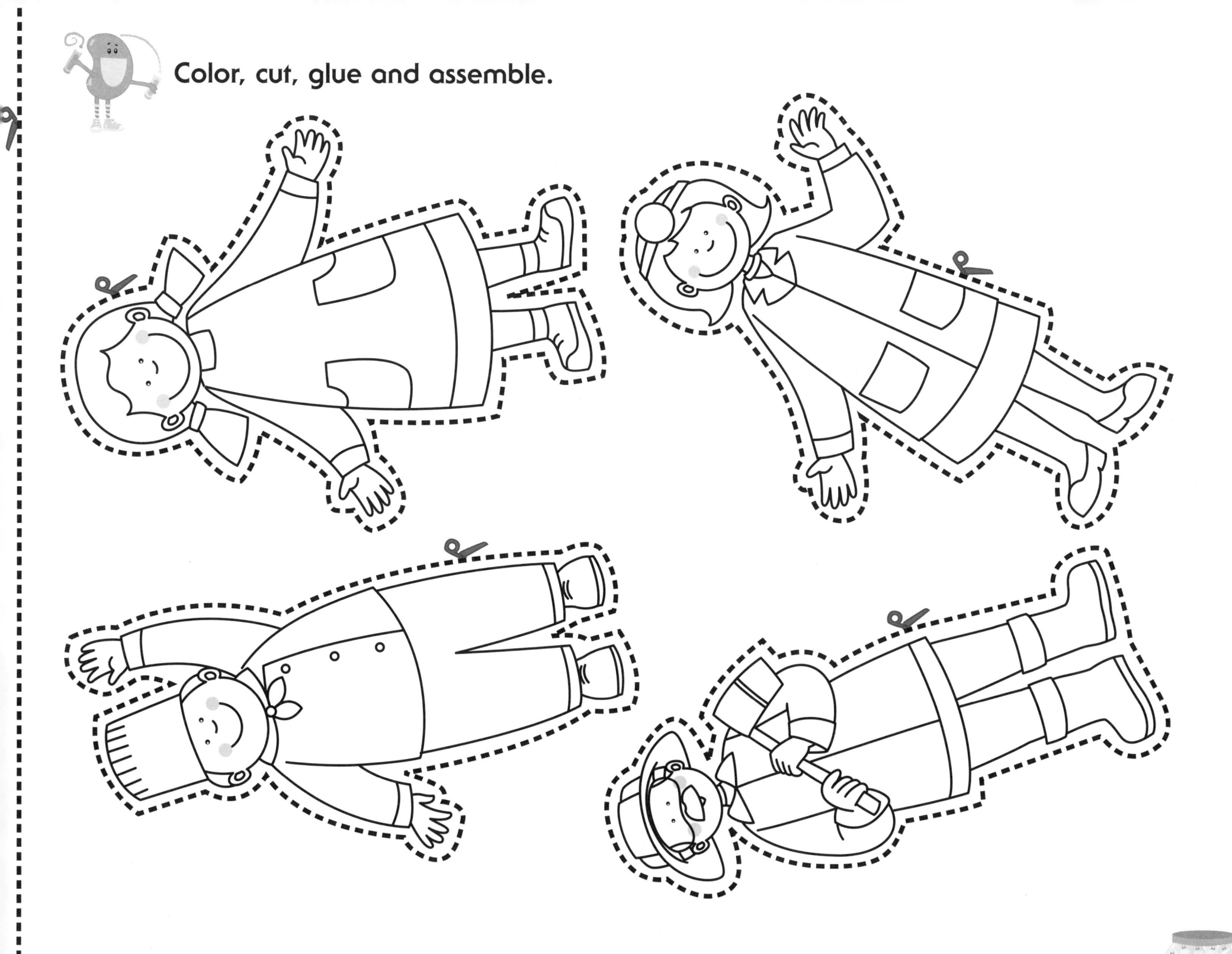

Jellybeans 3

Unit 6 **My town** Lesson 1

100 Unit 6 **My town** Lesson 1

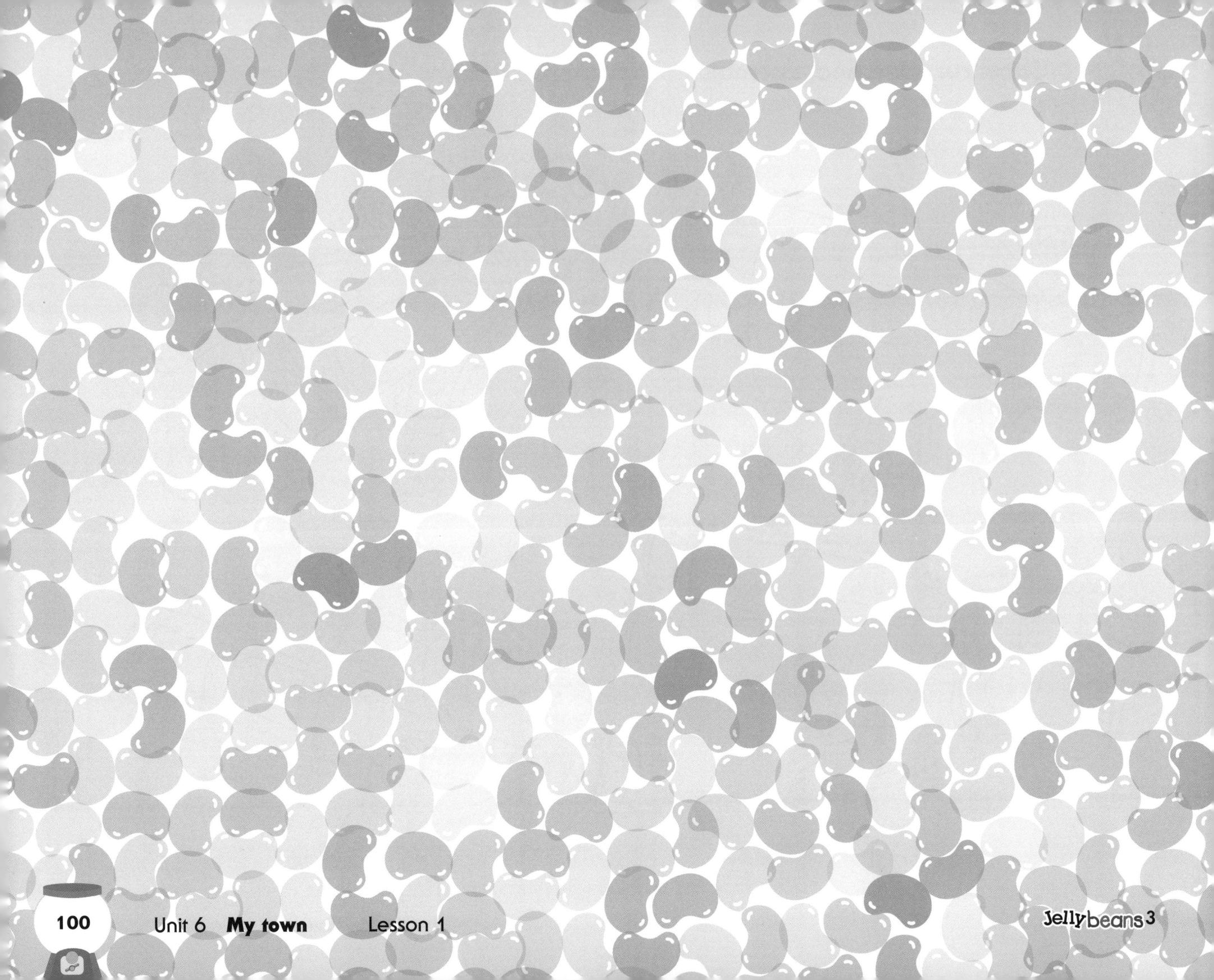

Color, finger-paint and cut.

Jellybeans 3

Unit 6 **My town** Lesson 1

101

102 Unit 6 **My town** Lesson 1

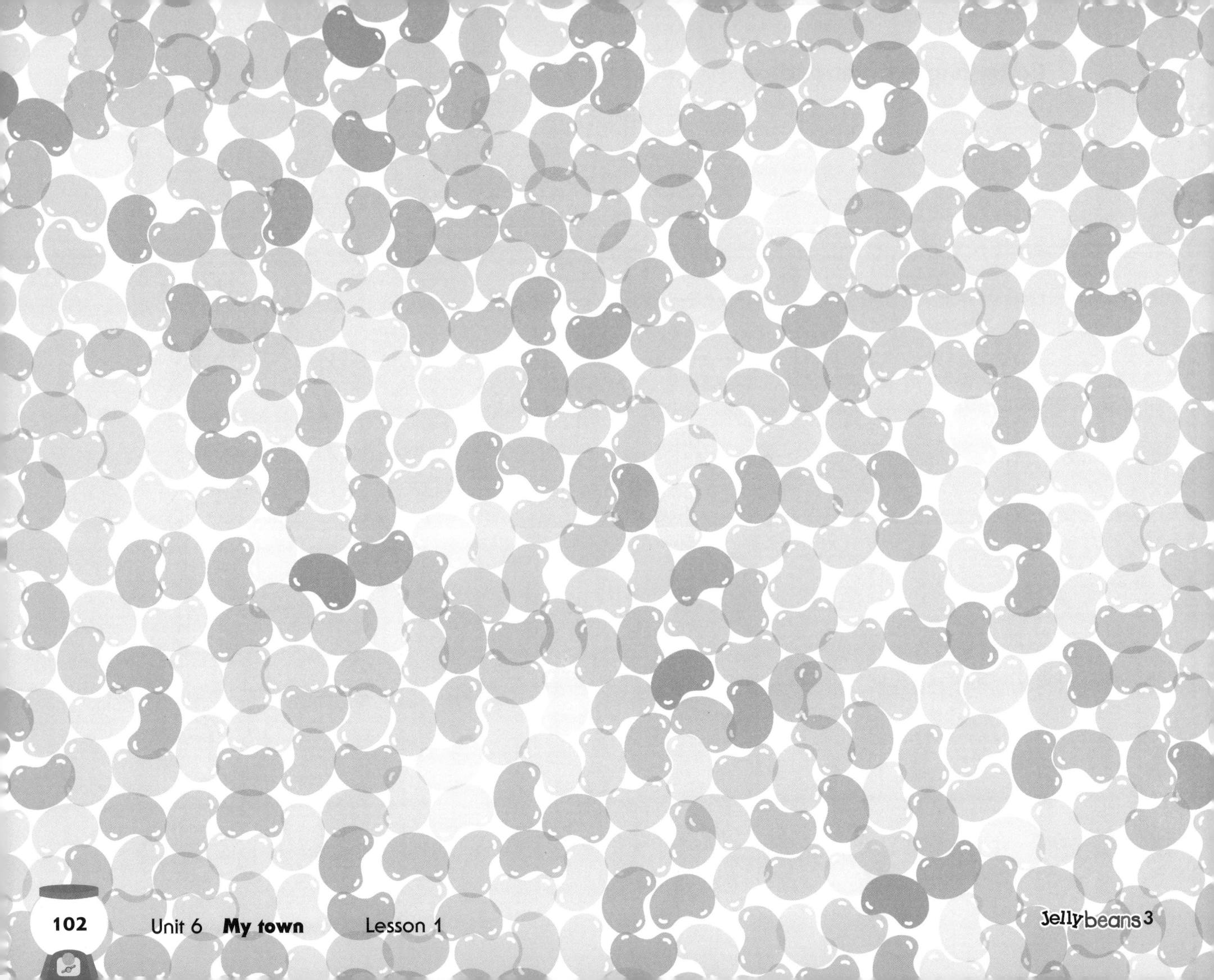

Paint, glue, cut and assemble.

Hospital

Bakery

Police Station

School

Restaurant

Fire Station

Jellybeans 3

Unit 6 **My town** Lesson 2

103

Unit 6 **My town** Lesson 2

Paint, cut, glue and assemble.

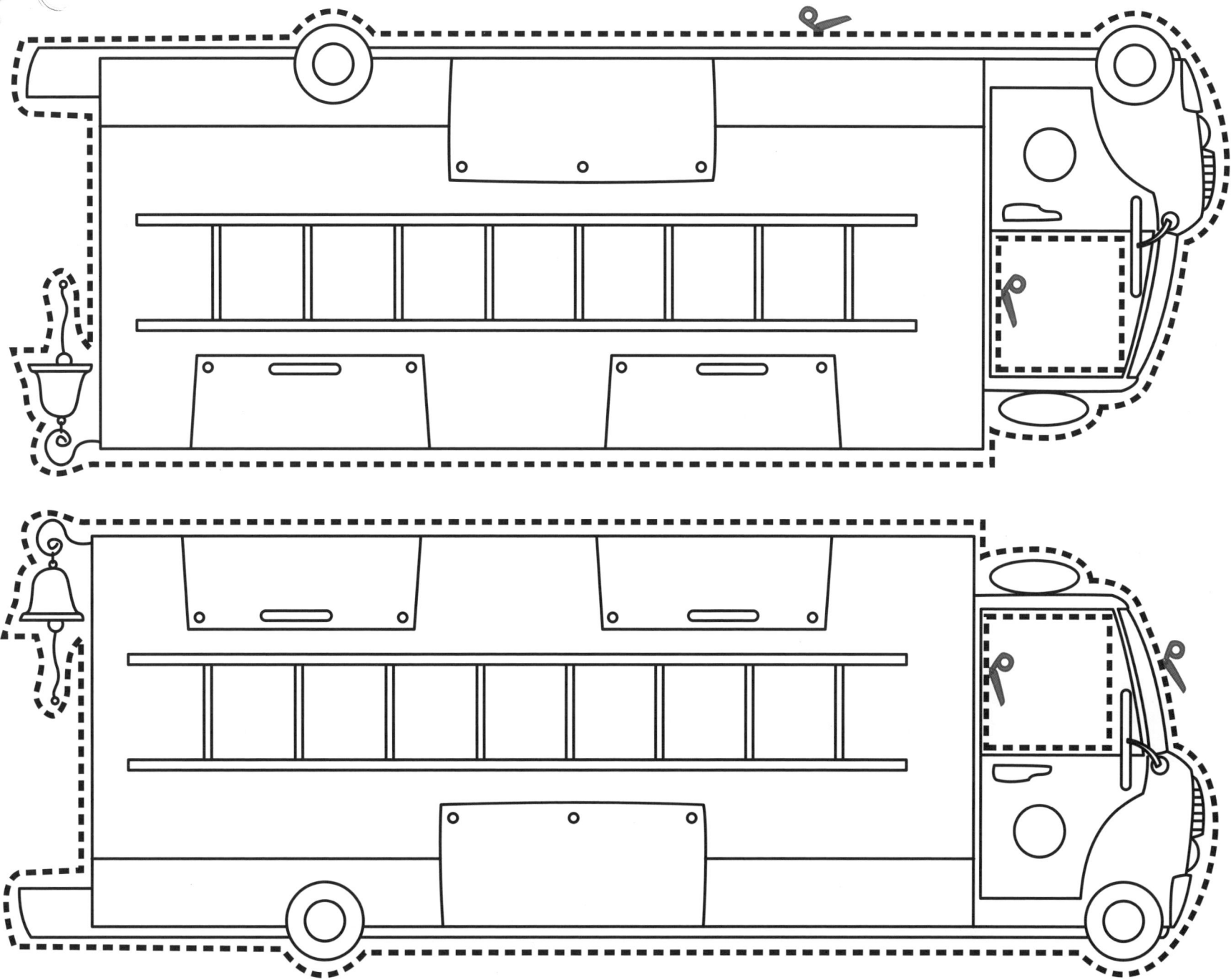

Unit 6 **My town** Lesson 2

Unit 6 **My town** Lesson 2

Color, glue, cut and assemble.

Unit 7 **At the zoo** Lesson 1

108 Unit 7 **At the zoo** Lesson 1

Jellybeans 3

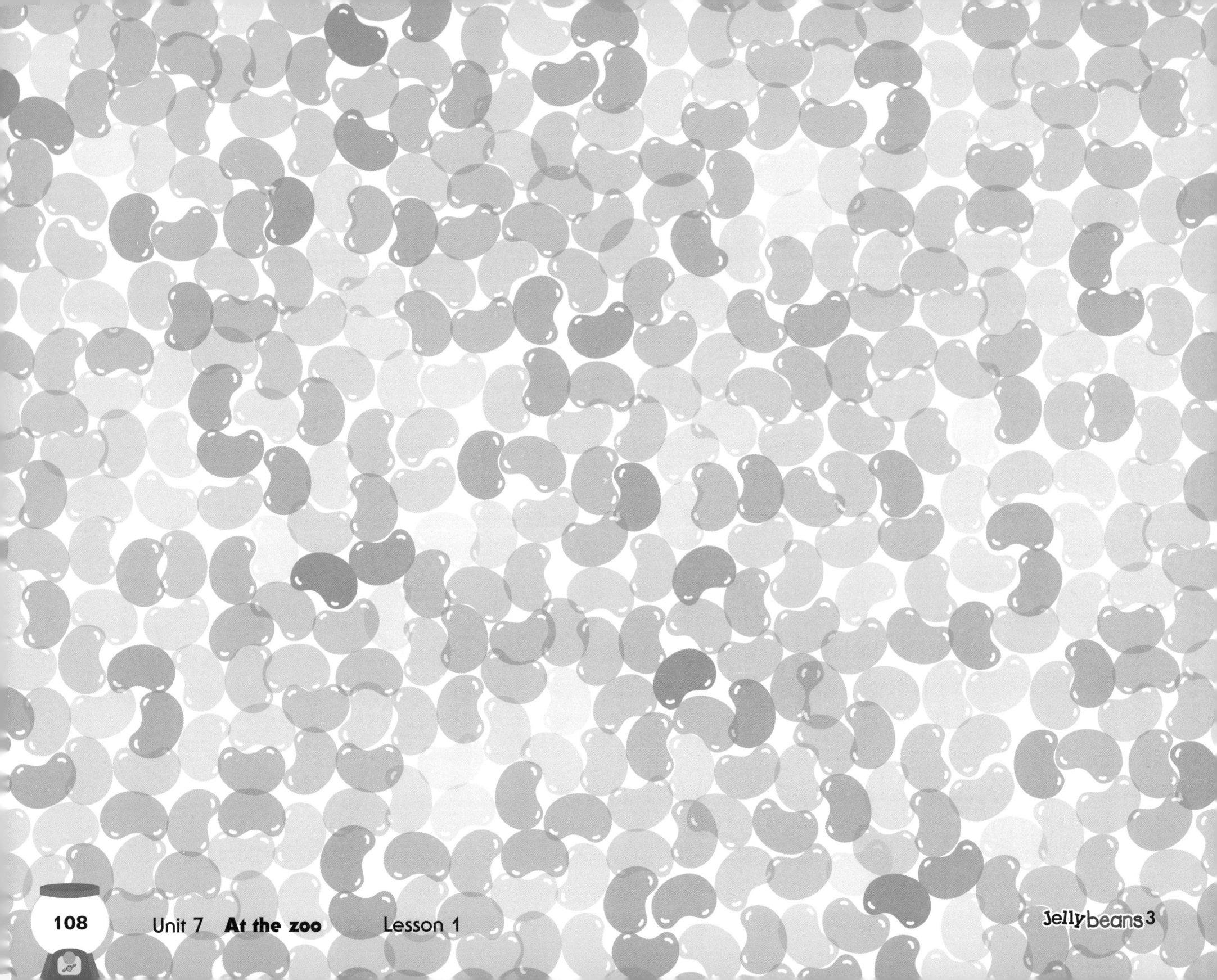

Paint, cut and assemble.

Jellybeans 3 — Unit 7 **At the zoo** — Lesson 1

Unit 7 **At the zoo** Lesson 1

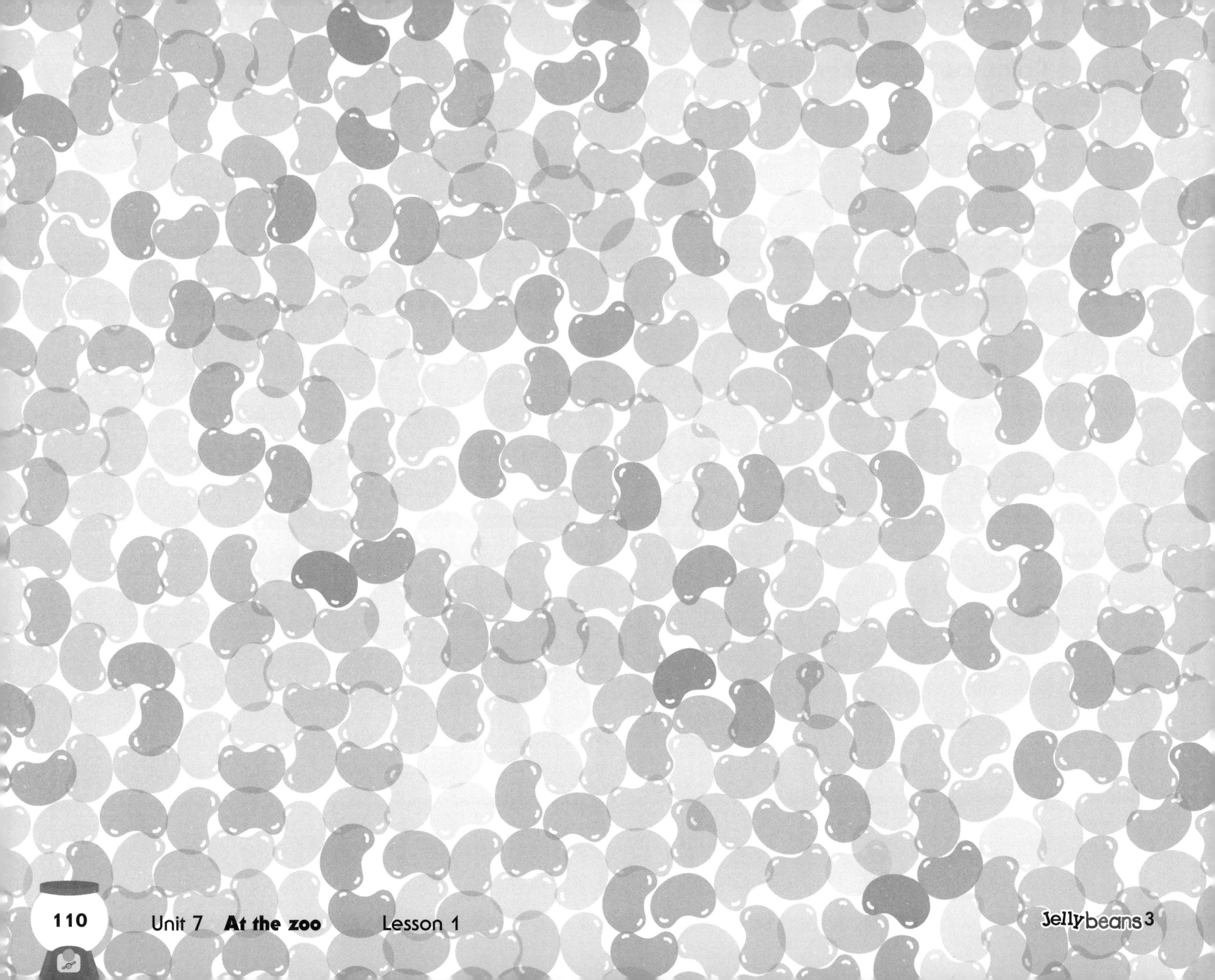

Color, cut and play.

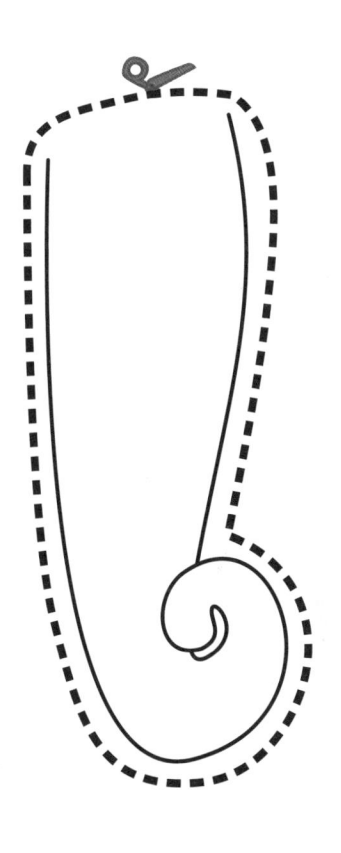

Jellybeans 3 · Unit 7 **At the zoo** · Lesson 2 · 111

112 Unit 7 **At the zoo** Lesson 2

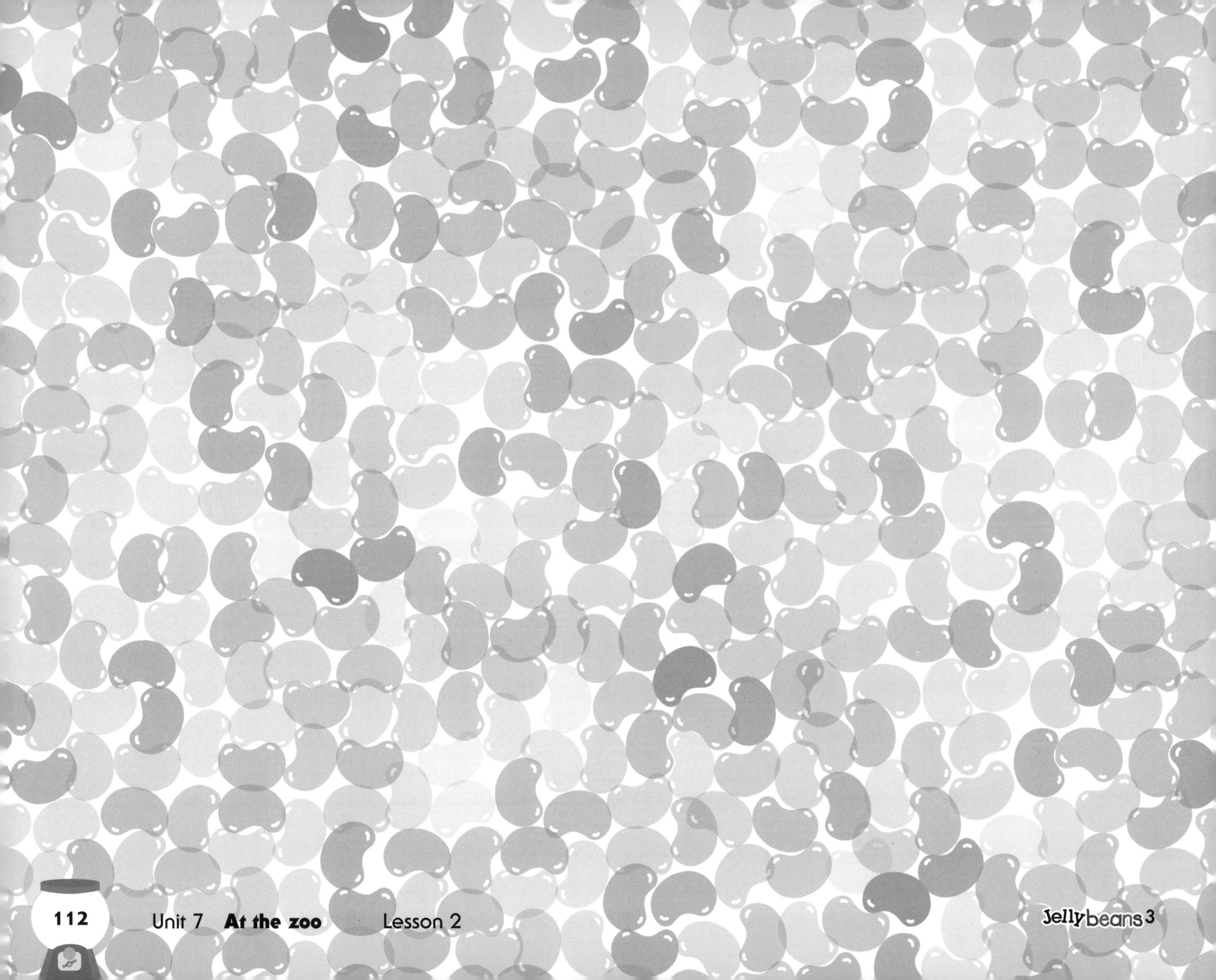

Color, paint, cut and assemble.

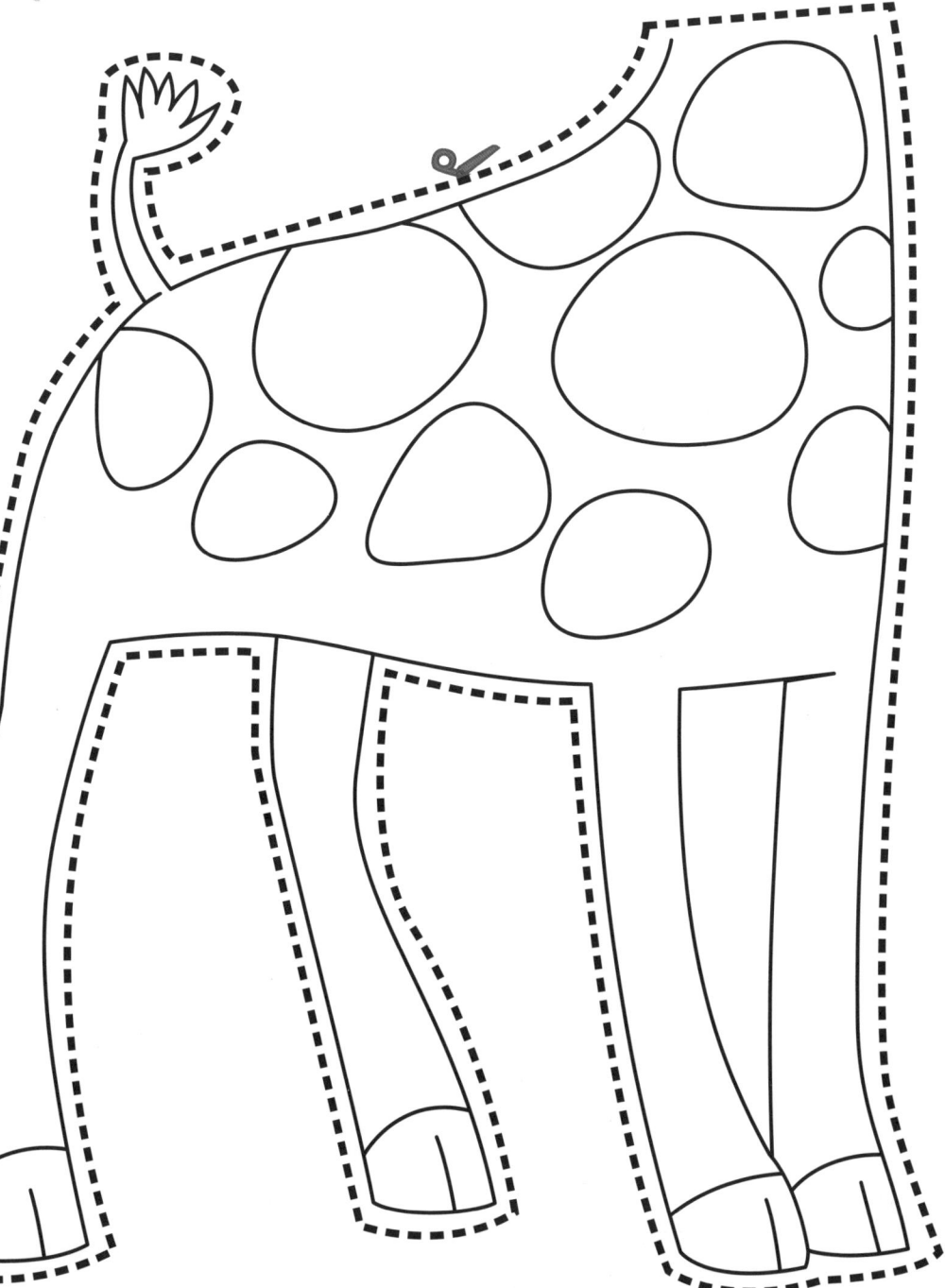

Jellybeans 3   Unit 7 **At the zoo**   Lesson 2   113

114   Unit 7   **At the zoo**   Lesson 2

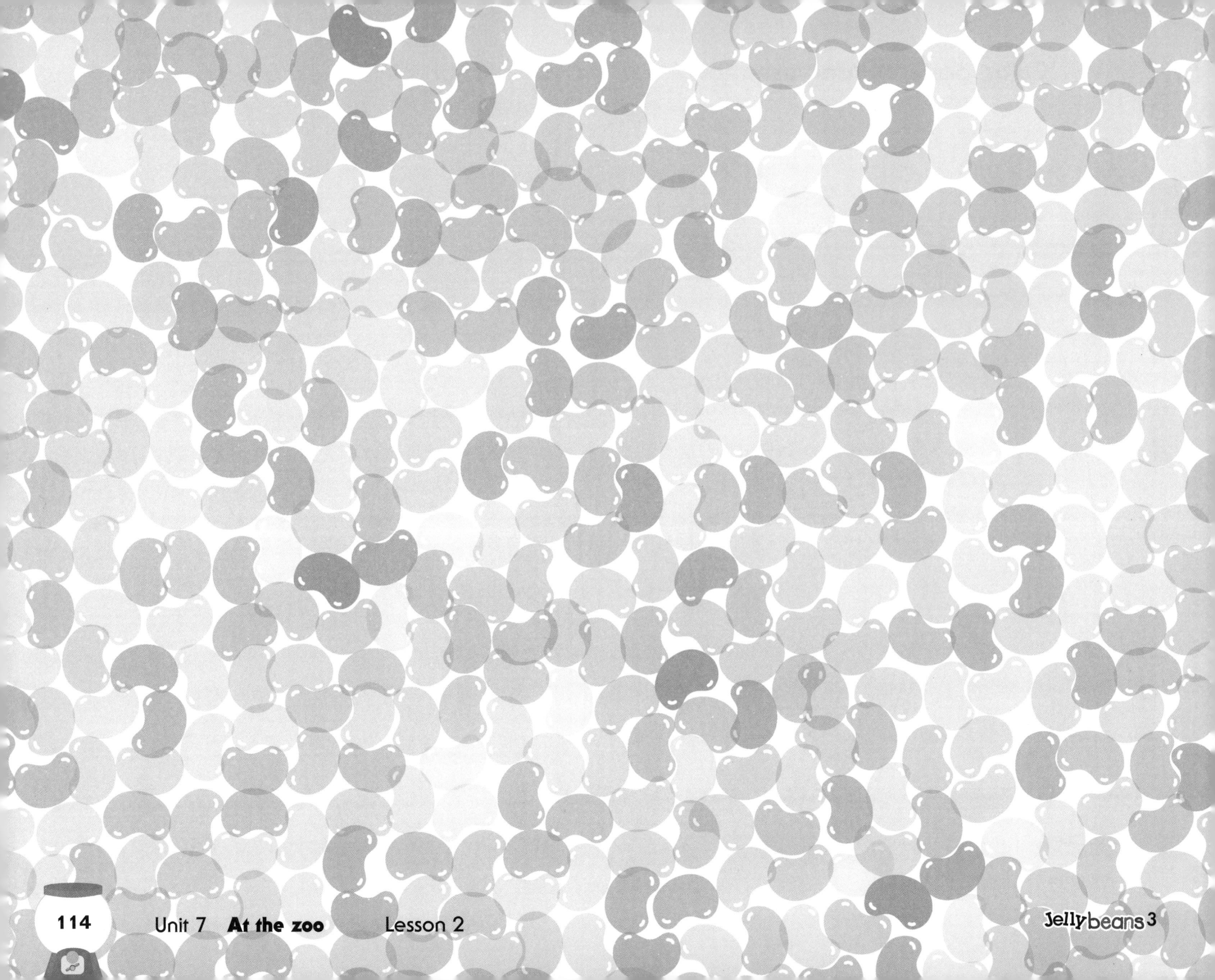

Color, glue, cut and assemble.

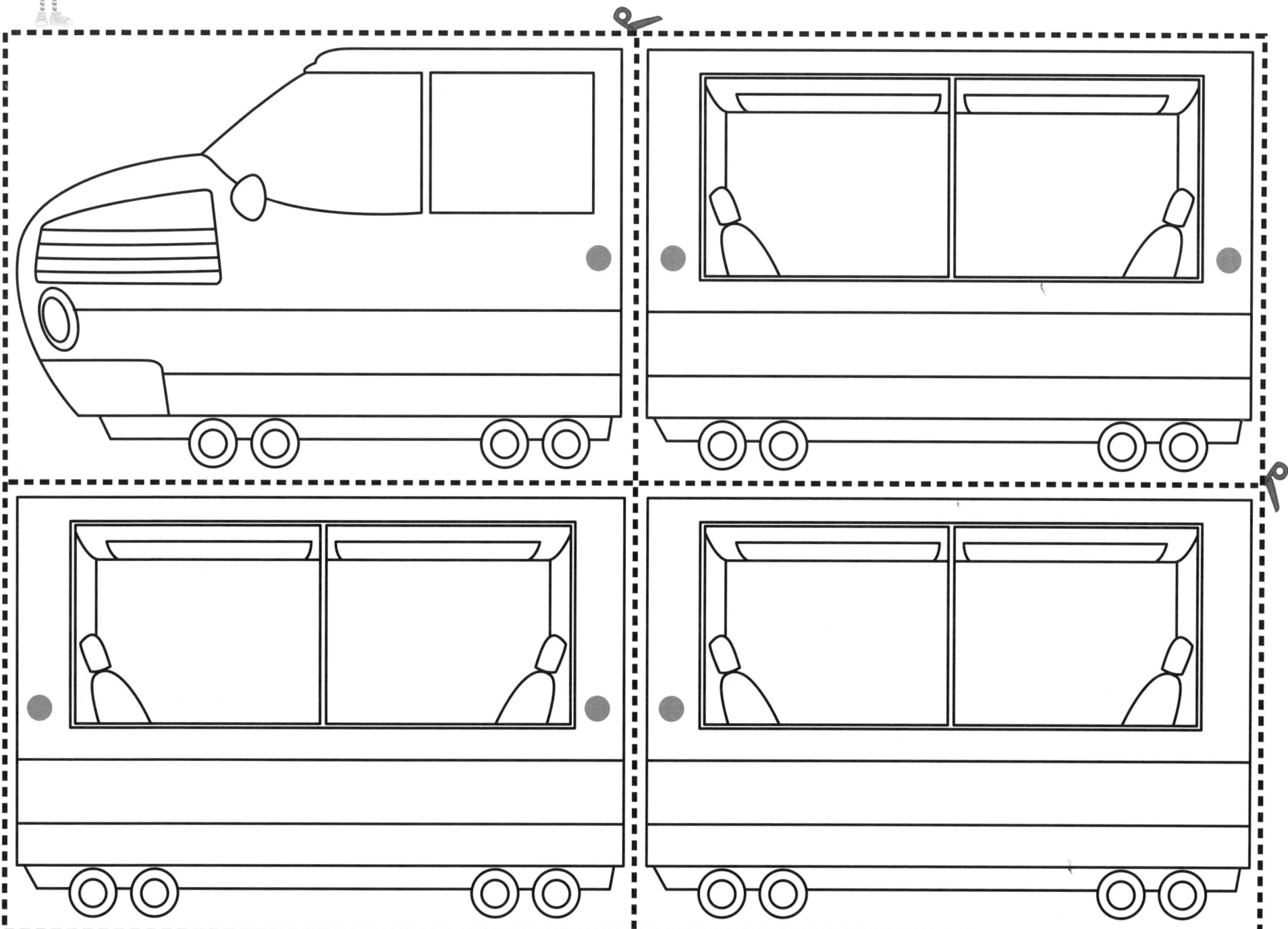

Jellybeans 3 — Unit 8 **Going places** — Lesson 1

116 Unit 8 **Going places** Lesson 1

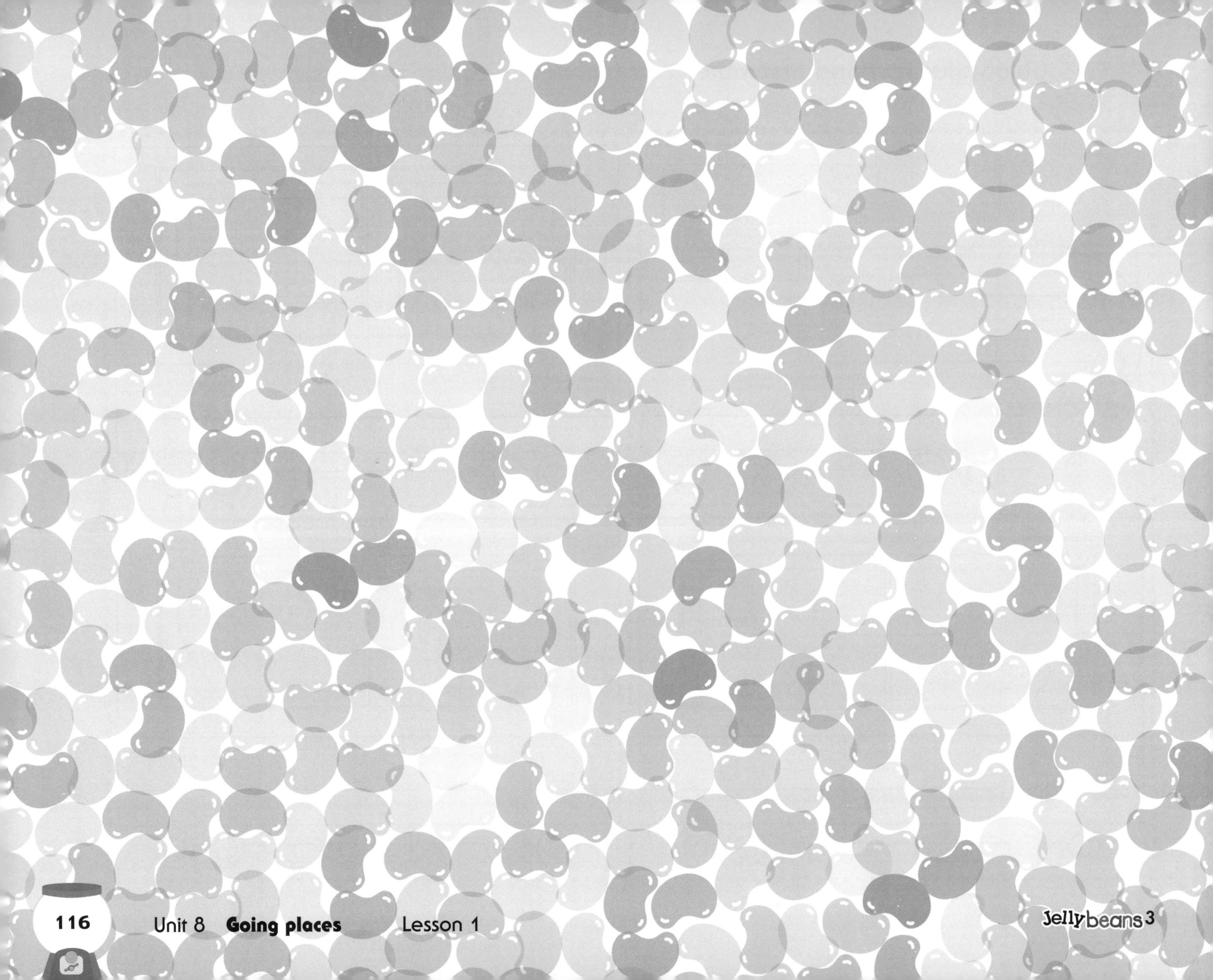

Finger-paint, cut and assemble.

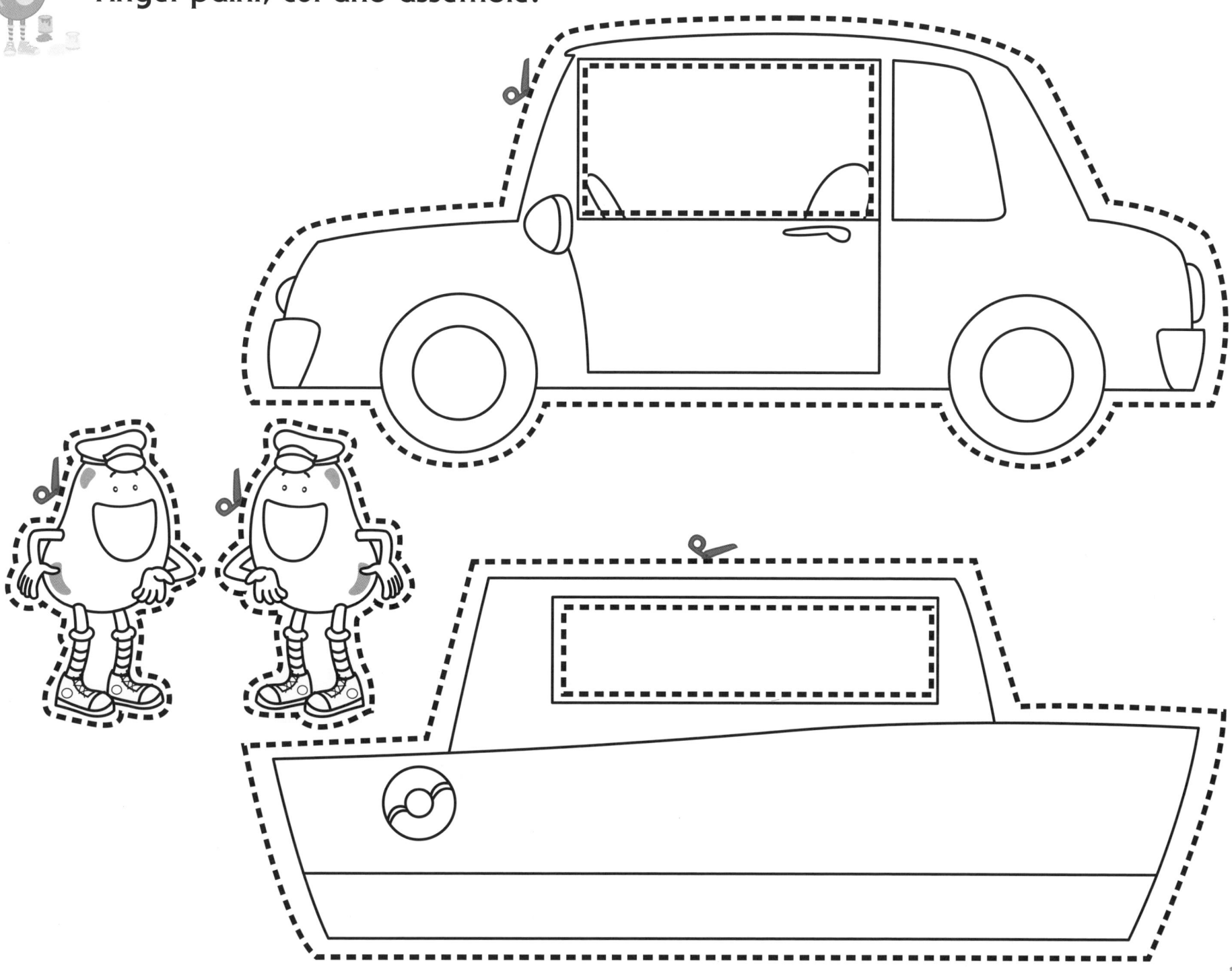

Jellybeans 3

Unit 8 **Going places** Lesson 1

117

Unit 8 **Going places** Lesson 1

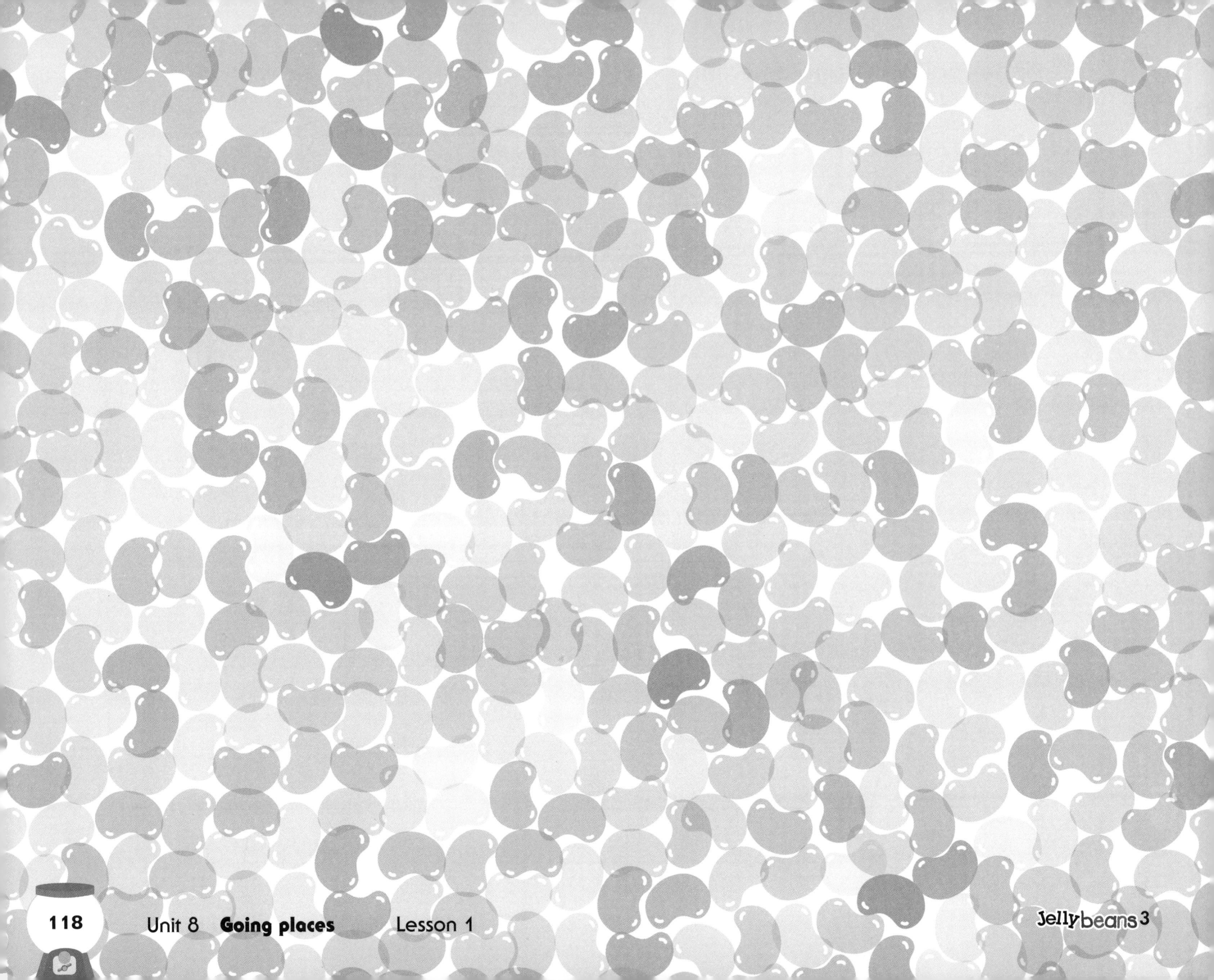

Paint, cut and assemble.

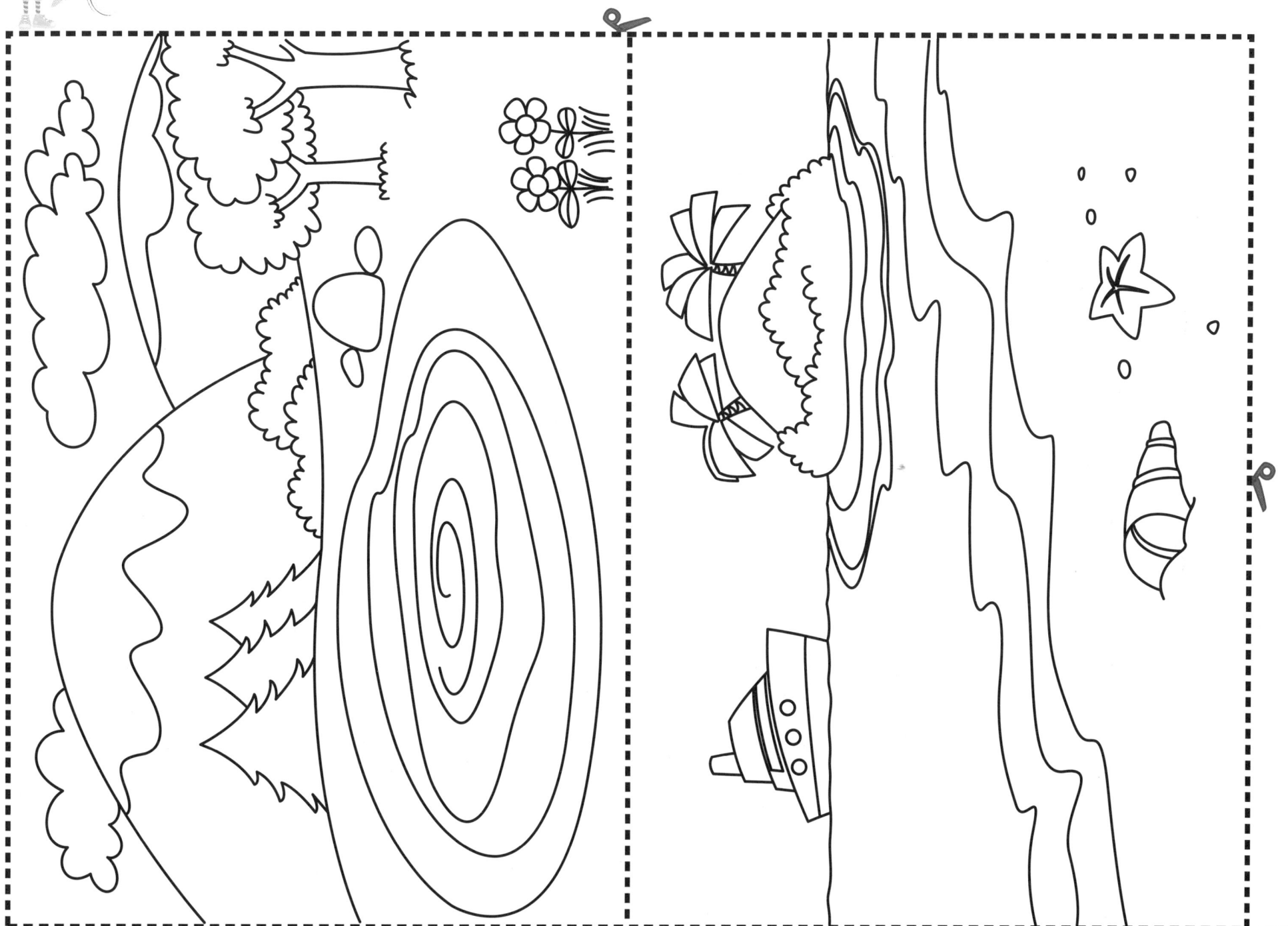

Jellybeans 3

Unit 8 **Going places** Lesson 2

119

Unit 8   **Going places**   Lesson 2

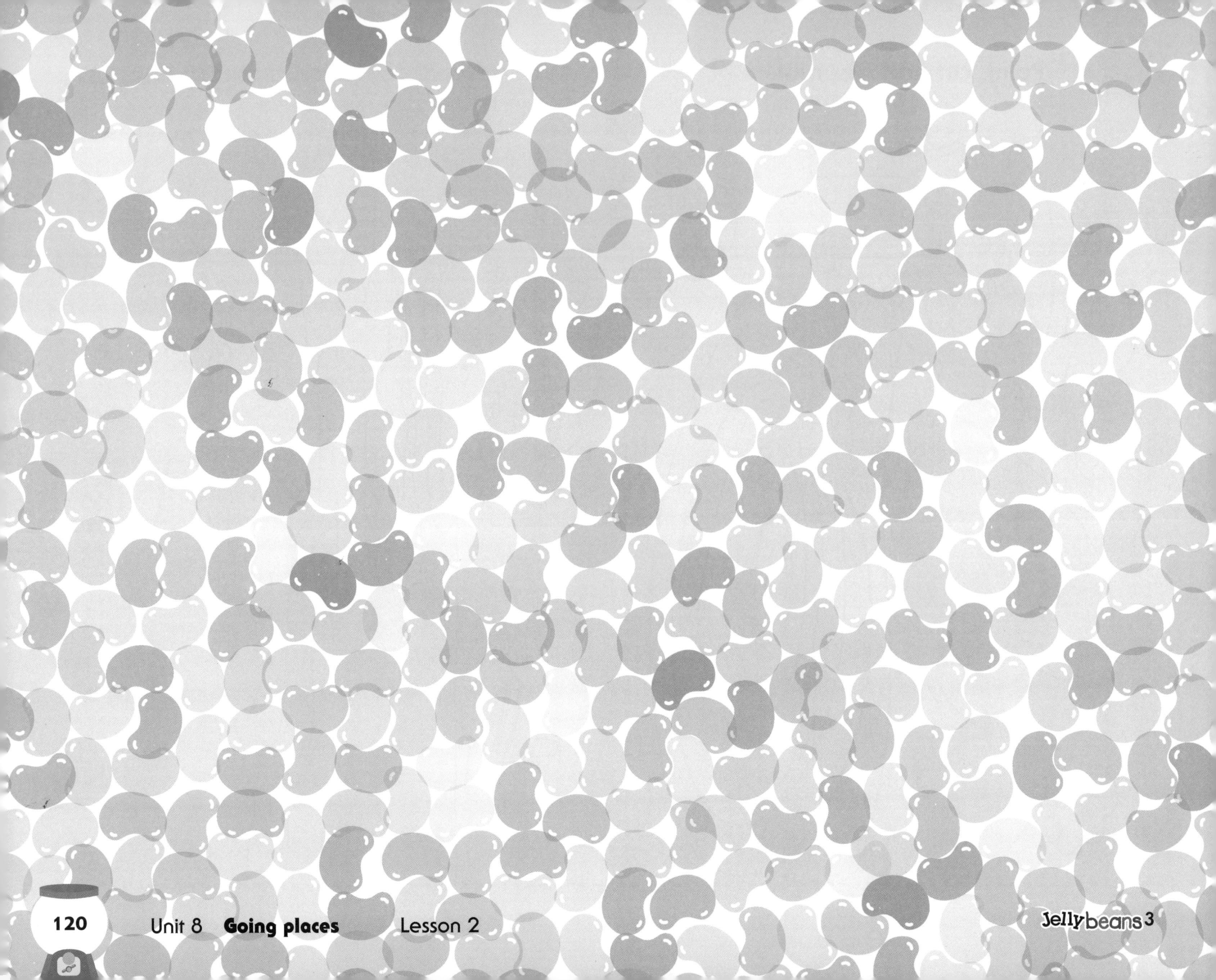

Color, draw, paint and glue.

Unit 8 **Going places** Lesson 2

122 Unit 8 **Going places** Lesson 2

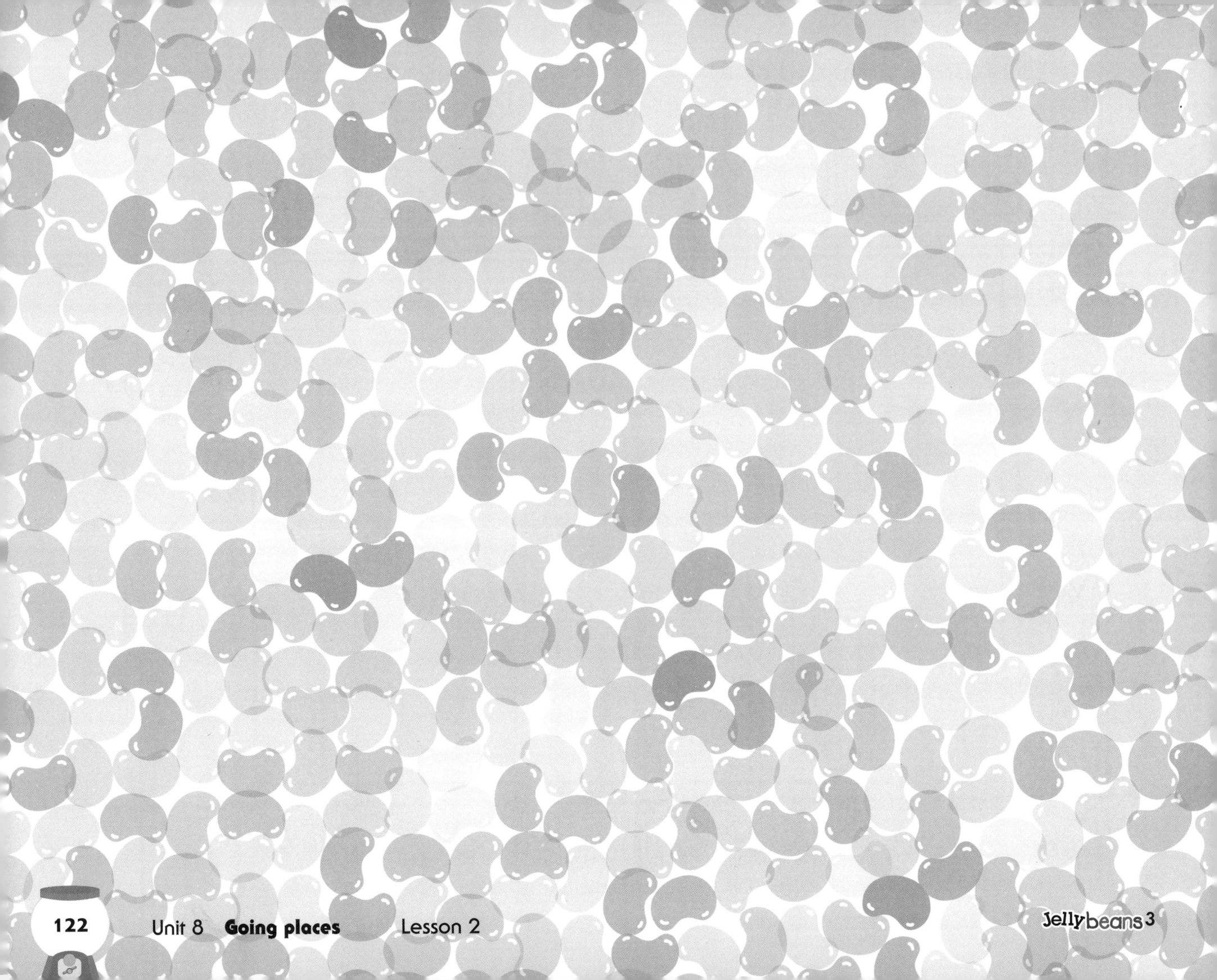

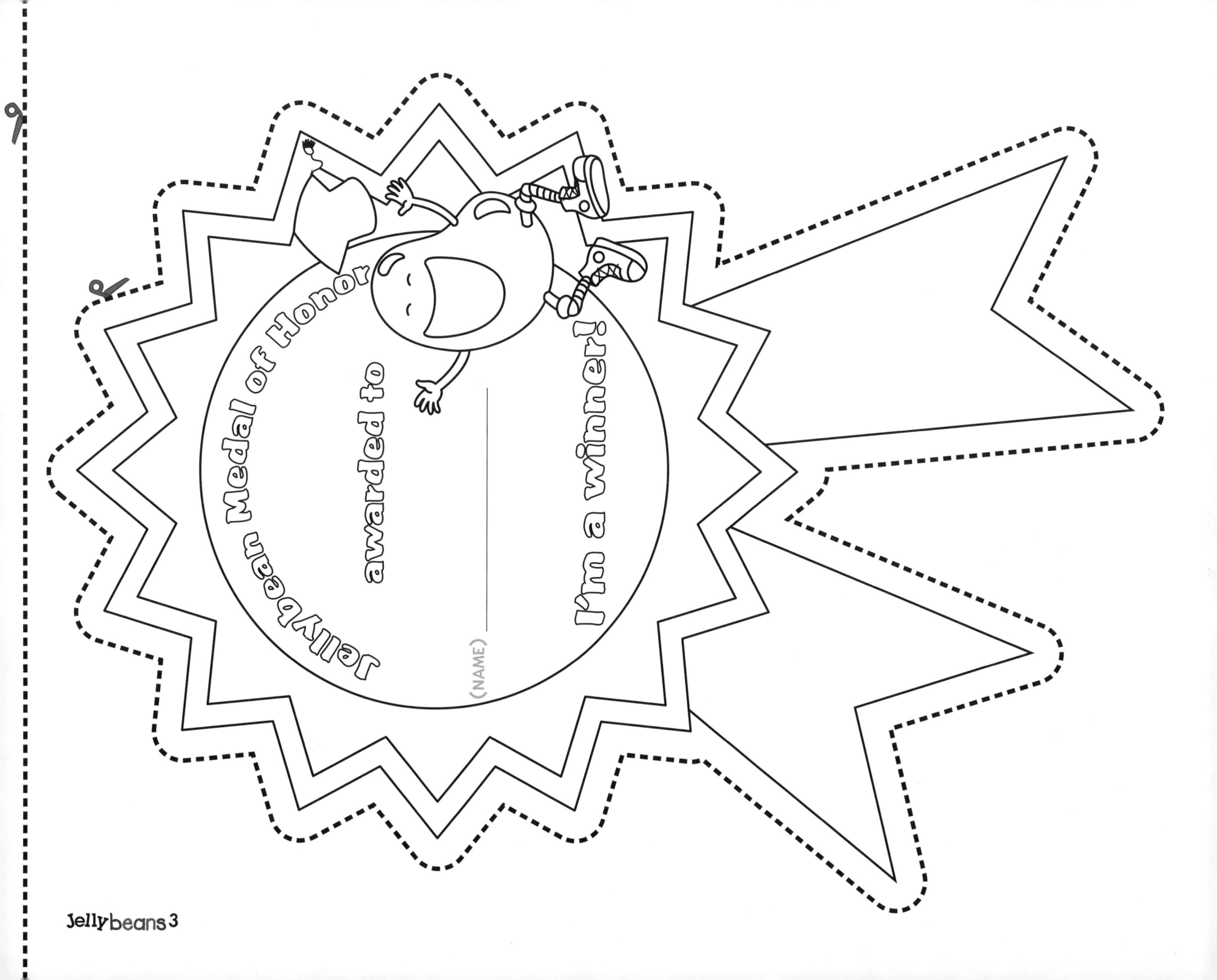

Jellybean Medal of Honor

awarded to
_____
(NAME)

I'm a winner!

Jellybeans 3

Jellybeans 3

Tracks

2	My friend is here today	17	I can be a helper
3	I color with my crayon	18	Nature song
4	I like to go to school	19	I love the mountains
5	Catching bugs	20	Up and down
6	We're going on a bug hunt	21	On the land
7	Head, shoulders, knees and toes	22	The worker's song
8	Hands on shoulders	23	I'm a little firefighter
9	Marching, marching	24	I'm a big police officer
10	Before I go to school	25	'Round the village
11	Wash your hands	26	What can you see?
12	Wash your face	27	The elephant
13	Coughs and sneezes	28	All kinds of animals
14	The family's in the house	29	The wheels on the bus
15	Sally go 'round the sun	30	Vacation time
16	Day or night?	31	Row your boat

Jellybeans 3

Jellybeans 3

RICHMOND
58 St. Aldates
Oxford, OX1 1ST
England

Publisher: *Alicia Becker*
Executive Editors: *Alejandra Zapiain, Kimberley Silver*
Proofreader: *Lawrence Lipson*

Design Supervisor and Art Direction: *Marisela Pérez*
Design: *Marilú Jiménez*
Cover Illustration: *Raúl García*
DTP and Layout: *Claudia Rocha, Patricia Lorenzana*
Technical Department: *Daniel Santillán, Edgar Colín, José Luis Ávila, Salvador Pereira*

Illustrations: *Carlos Vélez, Gerardo Vaca, Javier Montiel, Richard Zela, Rogelio Bonilla, Tania Juárez*

First Edition: D.R. © Richmond Publishing, S.A. de C.V., 2008

All rights reserved. No part of this book may be reproduced, stored in a retrieval system or transmitted in any form or by any means, electronic, mechanical, photocopying, recording or otherwise, without prior permission in writing of the publishers.

Every effort has been made to trace the owners of copyright, but if any omissions can be rectified, the publisher will be pleased to make the necessary arrangements.

This Edition: © Editora Moderna Ltda., 2011.
Editor: *Carla Montenegro*
Pedagogical Consultant: *Silvia Teles*
Copy Editor: *Sheila Winckler S. da Silva*
Proofreaders: *Adriana Cristina Bairrada, Camila Carmo da Silva, Mariana Mininel de Almeida, Vivian M. Viccino*
Designer: *Gláucia Koller*
Layout: *Yara Campi*
Impressão e Acabamento: *Gráfica RONA*
Lote: 768407
Cod: 24070779

Dados Internacionais de Catalogação na Publicação (CIP)
(Câmara Brasileira do Livro, SP, Brasil)

Salvador, Rebecca Williams
  Jelly beans, 3 : student's book / Rebecca Williams & Katy Smith. — São Paulo : Moderna, 2011.

  Suplementado pelo manual do professor

  1. Inglês (Educação infantil) I. Smith, Katy. II. Título.

11-04419   CDD-372.21

Índices para catálogo sistemático:
1. Inglês : Educação infantil   372.21

ISBN 978-85-16-07077-9 (LA)
ISBN 978-85-16-07078-6 (LP)

Reprodução proibida. Art.184 do Código Penal e Lei 9.610 de 19 de fevereiro de 1998.
Todos os direitos reservados.

RICHMOND
EDITORA MODERNA LTDA.
Rua Padre Adelino, 758 – Belenzinho
São Paulo – SP – Brasil – CEP 03303-904
Central de atendimento ao usuário: 0800 771 8181
www.richmond.com.br
2023

Impresso no Brasil

Jelly beans 3

Stickers

Jellybeans 3

Unit 1 I can do it

1

Unit 2　**One bug, two bugs**

Unit 3 **My healthy body**

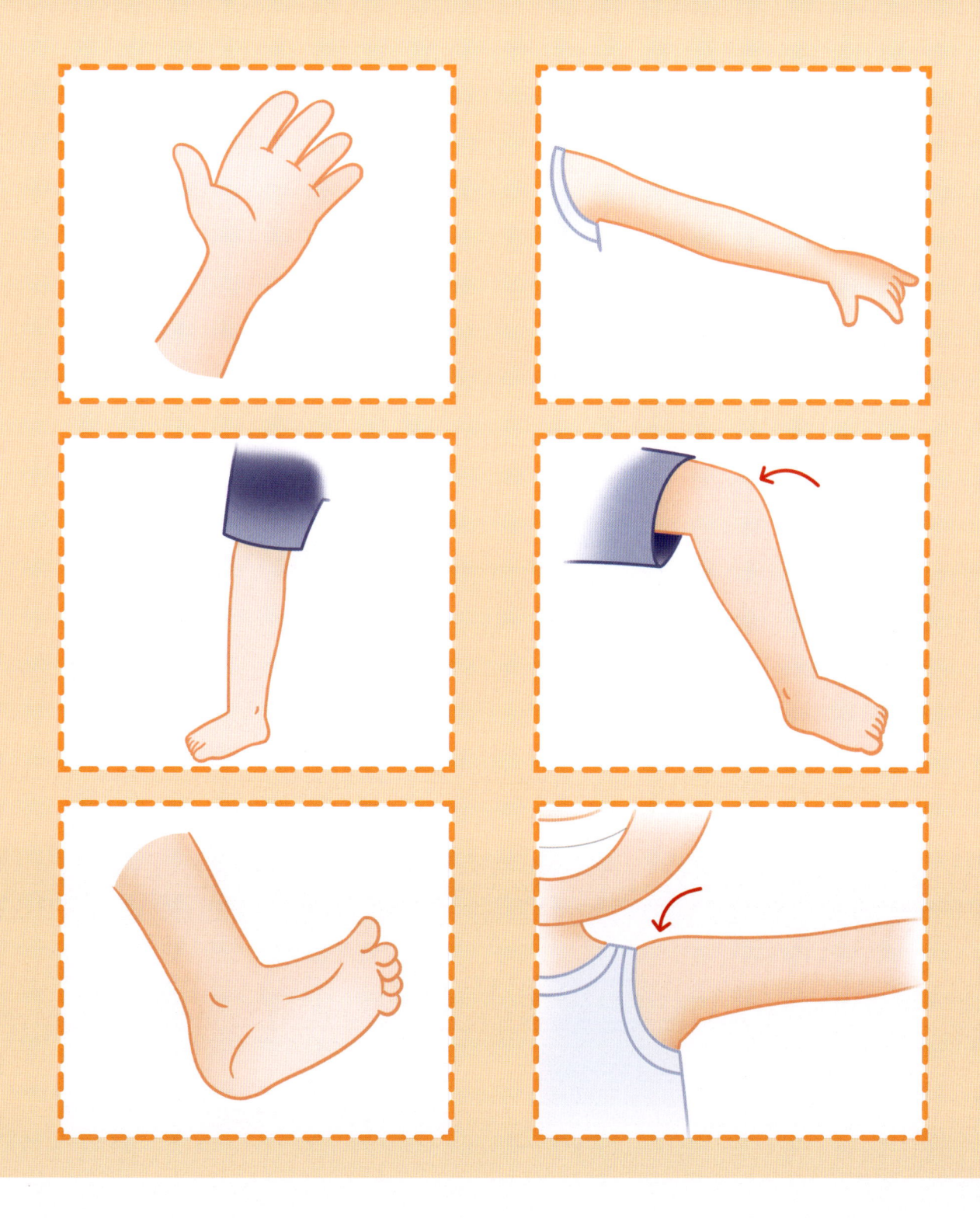

Unit 3 **My healthy body**

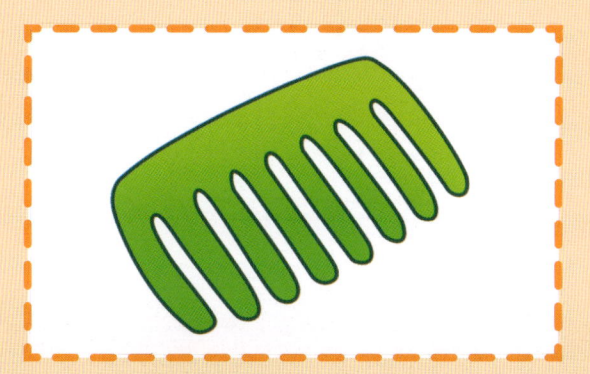

Unit 4   Busy days

Unit 5 My world

Unit 5   **My world**

Unit 6 **My town**

Unit 7 At the zoo

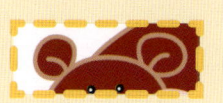

13

14

15

Unit 8 Going places